CAMERAS
OF THE PEOPLE'S REPUBLIC
OF CHINA

CAMERAS

OF THE PEOPLE'S REPUBLIC

OF CHINA

BY DOUGLAS ST DENNY

JESSOP
SPECIALIST
PUBLISHING

Cameras of The People's Republic of China
edited and designed by
Wordpower Books,
PO Box 303, Welwyn, Hertfordshire, AL6 9AG.

Production Editor: John Wade.

**Published by Jessop Specialist Publishing,
Jessop House,
98 Scudamore Road, Leicester, LE3 1TZ.
First published 1989.**

ISBN 0 9514392 0 0

Printed by Butler and Tanner Limited.,
Selwood Printing Works,
Frome, Somerset, BA11 1NF.

Acknowledgement

LIVING in a foreign country is never easy, and China is no exception. The language and customs work to isolate the inquiring foreigner.

This book could not have been possible without the help of Mr. Liu Bang, of the Chinese Photographers' Association. Through the offices of Liu Bang, I was able to make contact with camera manufacturers, and retired workers. He even acted as translator on more than one occasion.

Mr. Lin and Mr. Jia of International Photography magazine were always available. When they said that they would try to find the answer to a particularly sticky question, they found it. Xiao Jia (xiao meaning little, but a term of address used by an older person for a younger) worked very hard making simultaneous translations of my lectures. He even kept the punch lines in jokes so they brought a chuckle to the Chinese audience.

Yu Dong Shui is supposed to be a student of the Hindi language, but he found time to be my secretary, and all-round gofer. He wore the same smiling face whether translating a letter from a camera owner in Hohehot, or washing our jeep in preparation for a trip into the city.

In the middle of writing this book, we were blessed with the birth of Emily Flore. She slowed the process, but never kept it from rolling forward.

Most of all, it was my wife, Marie-Christine who made this book happen. She took over many of the everyday chores, in addition to her teaching schedule, and the care and feeding of Emily. She always encouraged me, and never complained when I needed to travel for a few days, looking for a camera, or meeting a 'camera' friend. She always had a cup of tea ready for the unexpected Chinese visitor, and did her best to take messages in Chinese over the phone. Without her, this would have not been possible.

This book is dedicated to two very important men in my life:
my father, Raymond D. St Denny, who taught me
I could do anything in life I wanted to do,
and Gene Collard, who taught me about cameras
and what to do with them!

Contents

Foreword

By Michael Pritchard, FRPS

Photographic Specialist, Christie's, London

CAMERAS AND PHOTOGRAPHICA are a relatively new, but already, well-established, area for collectors. Since 1971 there has been a steady rise in interest and a growing number of collectors worldwide.

It is inevitable that once a collector's field develops and matures then individual collectors will begin to specialise. Particular makes, types of camera, age of cameras or other criteria will often govern how a collection is assembled. On the other hand, some collectors, while claiming not to specialise, will just collect the camera that they actually discover within the limits of their own leisure time.

There are pros and cons to forming a specialist collection. Except when funds and display space are unlimited, a focus in a particular direction will often result in a more interesting and worthwhile collection.

A New Area of Collecting

Douglas St Denny, at a stroke with this book, has identified and set the parameters for a whole new area of collecting that has hitherto not been approached: that of the Chinese cameras. A whole new area has been clearly defined for the collector that is small enough to allow individuals to build up a complete or representative collection, but with enough variety to make it attractive. The field also contains a mix of relatively common and rare models to give the

A familiar sight for the Chinese camera collector - the street scene in front of Cai Shi Kai secondhand store, the place where many of the cameras in this book were found.

collector the excitement of the hunt that represents so much of the joy of camera collecting.

The Chinese camera industry as a large-scale operation is new compared with that of England, France or the United States. This adds interest for the collector and St Denny has captured the whole known production history of an entire country's camera-making industry. He has been able to contact many of the people originally involved with camera production in order to collect and check information.

The Language Problem

The problems involved with this have been immense. The language problem has meant reliance on interpreters with their own interpretation of words and editing of speech and documentary evidence likewise has needed translation. The learning of basic Chinese writing and reading skills has been necessary to seek out sources of information.

The Chinese, by nature, are secretive and the effects of the 1949 and Cultural Revolutions have meant that people have been reluctant to talk to foreigners - particularly on technical matters. In some cases, details of production and variations in production runs have been destroyed.

Nevertheless, St Denny has built up local contacts and cultivated them to ascertain information. The physical size of a country like China and the location of manufacturing plants has necessitated a great deal of travelling to track down special pieces of information for the book.

Despite all of these difficulties, St Denny has written a comprehensive and definitive book that is set to remain a standard work for the foreseeable future. The Chinese camera industry encompasses a range of cameras from Leica copies, 35mm cameras, twin lens reflexes and field cameras, amongst others, which provides the collector with a wide range of types to collect within the overall field.

The publication of St Denny's book will undoubtedly give an impetus to a new field of camera collecting and add to the known history of one country's camera industry.

Michael Pritchard

The Xing Fu, or 'Happiness' in English. The only known example of a true box camera, produced in China. Lack of interest from the public, however, meant a short life for this model.

Introduction

GUIDE BOOKS FOR the camera collector abound. However, there has never before been a guide book written about the cameras of the People's Republic of China.

After more than three years of visiting camera factories, talking to the people involved in making and selling cameras in China, making friends with local collectors and having articles published in the Chinese photo press, I have finally been able to put down on paper, a short course in Chinese cameras.

I have made very little effort to write about the European cameras brought into China in the 1920s and 1930s by the foreigners who lived and worked here. A few European manufacturers had offices here, and sold their cameras directly on the Chinese market. Zeiss, Leitz, Kodak and some others all have left their marks, which still show up from time to time on Chinese second-hand store shelves.

Slightly more thought has been put into describing the result of the influence of the Eastern Bloc countries, whose technicians and technology allowed the Chinese Camera Industry to get off the ground.

Prices for cameras are given in RMB yuan, literally People's Money. At the time of writing (February 1989) the official exchange rate is $1 (US) to 3.71 RMB yuan. On the black market the rate can be twice this. It must be kept in mind that a Chinese factory worker today may make as much as 200 RMB yuan a month, and he pays rent of 2 RMB yuan per month for his apartment. A university professor makes about 110 RMB yuan a month, and a beginning high school teacher gets 56 RMB yuan. All three get additional help from the government by way of subsidised prices for meat, rice, oil and flour.

This book is not meant to contain every camera made in China.

Firstly, many of the twin lens reflex cameras made during the 1960s and 1970s look alike, and indeed, except for the location of the factory and the name plates, they are clones of the Seagull 4-B TLR.

Secondly, just after I have decided that I have a complete list, it seems another camera pops up. Even the Chinese themselves cannot agree on how many camera models have been produced.

Chinese names are often written in characters. In writing this book, every effort has been made to make a faithful translation of the meaning of the original Chinese. In order to give the reader a taste of the sound of these words, the Pinyin system of romanization has been used for all Chinese characters. This method of printing words has been chosen by the Chinese Government as the official way. It might also be noted that place names are designated in the same system. The Peking of the 1920s is the Beijing of today.

Any errors in this book are of my own doing, and the reader is requested to bring them to my attention. Question marks are used next to information of an unconfirmed nature. This information is generally an intelligent estimate, or an extrapolation based on talking to people who cannot agree on dates or figures. A question mark standing alone indicates that the information is simply not available.

Douglas St Denny

Camera production past and present

ACCORDING TO CHINESE history, Zou Boqi (1819-1869), from southern Guangdond province, invented photography. He made *'... an apparatus for taking pictures...'* in 1844. He left behind his notes and, after his death, plans for making various photographic devices as well as formulae for making light-sensitive material were found among them. It is also said that he left behind a photograph of himself. It is not mentioned, however, if this photo was the result of his own efforts, or if it was made by one of the European methods of photography then current.

Also in 1844, during the Qing dynasty, a government official named Qi Ying gave portraits of himself to representatives of England, France, Portugal, and the United States. His portrait was discovered by M. Fage, curator of the French Museum of Photography in 1968. It was in amongst some 35 other daguerreo-types taken by Jules Itier, the French Inspector of Customs in China during the mid 1800s.

M. Itier took quite a few photographs in Guangzhou, Macao and Hong Kong. Much of his work was published, and some of his photographs were printed in the *History of French Photography* printed in 1920.

Photography was the activity of the wealthy foreign population. The mer-chants, bankers, and diplomats who lived in the open cities of China had the time and the money to indulge themselves in what was a rather expensive hobby. The general Chinese population remained ignorant of the photographic process until after the 1911 revolution, which overthrew the rule of the Qing Emperor.

During the great construction projects of the turn of the century, Chinese photographers were sent to document the building of factories, rail lines, roads, and mines. These pictures were then presented in album form to the Emperor, so that he could see the progress being made in his country.

Though these photographs, taken by Chinese photographers, show much of what was happening in China at that time, most of the photo history of everyday life was the result of camerawork by foreigners.

Zeiss was one manufacturer who made special efforts to fill the needs of the Chinese market. Above left is a Zeiss Super Ikonta stamped 'For China' and, in Chinese characters, 'German Product'. Below is the inside of another Zeiss camera, the Adoro Tropen, stamped with the words 'For China'.

In 1873, the British photographer John Thomson published a book called *Illustrations of China and Its People*. This book contained more than 200 photographs taken by him in China.

The European Presence

The Europeans and Americans who were taking pictures in China at that time brought their own equipment with them and it is certain that many of these wooden cameras suffered from both the journey, and the climate. The cameras which survived returned, no doubt, home with their owners. The cameras which didn't make the voyage home were probably used to heat the evening meal in some lucky Chinese family.

The design of these cameras was almost certainly copied by Chinese craftsmen, and locally made wooden cameras must have been made, though none have been found.

The influence of western civilization in China is evident throughout Chinese history and the history of cameras in China is no exception. The European population of China during the first quarter of this century brought with them their folding Kodaks and Zeiss plate cameras. The demand for photographic equipment by both foreign and upper class Chinese was so great that some camera manufacturers opened representative offices in the larger Chinese

The Polish Start, a twin lens reflex from the 1950s, found in China.

cities. Leitz, for example, had branches in Beijing, Shanghai, Tianjin, Hong Kong, Hankou, Nanjing, Harbin, and Mukden.

Zeiss made special efforts to fill the needs of the Chinese market. Today it is not too uncommon for a collector in the west to come across a Zeiss camera marked *For China.* Many German cameras sold in China in the 1930s bear the Chinese characters *German Product* engraved into their metal.

Russia has always been an influence on the Chinese camera industry. Left is a Russian Zenit 4, rare in the west. Below is the Yangtze River, a Chinese copy of the Russian Smena. Note the upside down 'U' on the lens at about 6 o'clock, meaning that this lens is coated.

Japan also left its mark with cameras from the 1930s and 1940s. China suffered under the occupation of Japanese troops from 1937 until 1945 and some of those troops left behind cameras which they brought with them from their home islands.

Japanese and German influences

Even before that, Japan was also one of the foreign powers, along with England, France, Russia, and Germany, holding special rights to Treaty Ports on the coast, and along the Yangtze River. Japanese plate cameras equipped with German lenses and shutters can still be found occasionally.

Folding cameras such as the Semi First and Marble are sometimes also seen on second-hand store shelves. Recently, a dealer from Hong Kong

Above: A Zenit SLR from Russia that was an obvious influence on the Chinese Zi Jin Shan (below). Like older Leicas, this camera uses the M39x1 screw mount, but with a lens-to-film plane distance that is longer than that found on the Leica.

picked up a Hansa Canon in Beijing. Wars and civil unrest have done much to deplete the supply of foreign cameras left in China. As late as the Cultural Revolution (1966-76) cameras of Western manufacture or design were systematically destroyed by the zealous Red Guards.

During the late 1970s, I am told that second-hand store shelves were well stocked with Leicas and Super Ikontas. It seems that these cameras were bought by visiting Japanese and Hong Kong businessmen. The population was afraid of another Cultural Revolution, and wanted to turn their foreign cameras into cash before they were forced to throw them into the lake, as many had been forced to do just a few years before.

Today, Chinese photographers and camera collectors value cameras like the Leica IIIc and IIIf much more highly than do collectors in the West. I was recently offered a Leica IIIc for the sum of 10,000 US$ I did not buy it.

Collectable Chinese cameras, however, appear to have little or no value to the Chinese themselves. Secondhand stores refuse to handle the Chinese cameras of the late fifties because they cannot make much profit on them.

A friend in Shanghai recently wrote and told me that he saw a very rare Serve The People 207 Polaroid copy for sale for only 12 RMB yuan. He didn't know that I wanted it, so he didn't buy it for me. Maybe it will come up for sale again someday, and if it does, I hope that I can afford to buy it.

Big and Little Brothers

Though the Chinese made copies of Leica cameras and Japanese cameras, most of the design work and manufacturing technology for the early Chinese industry came from the Soviet Union and its Eastern Bloc partners. Russia was known as China's Big Brother, while East Germany and the other Warsaw Pact countries were Little Brothers.

Almost from the beginning of the Communist movement in China, Chinese have been going to the Soviet Union to study. While they were there, they invariably picked up locally-made cameras. After liberation in 1949, a large influx of technicians from Russia, East Germany, Czechoslovakia and Poland arrived to help their Little Brother establish a new social system. With them came cameras made in their homelands.

Trade was soon established with these countries and soon afterwards, Chinese factories were making goods for export to Eastern Europe. Evidence exists to show that many of the thermoplastic cameras made in China in the late 1950s and early 1960s were made from moulds used for the same style cameras in Russia and Czechoslovakia. It is possible that the lenses for these cameras were imported from these two countries because China didn't have the facilities for grinding quality optics on a production scale.

Another explanation of the inverted 'U' to indicate lens coating is the readiness of the Chinese to use things foreign, in this case the Cyrillic letter used by their

The Russian Fed, a copy of the Leica IIIa, both of which were strong influences on the Chinese industry.

Russian Big Brothers. The same phenomenom exists today with the use of English.

Wang Bao Ruo (Jean Pasqualini) in his book *Prisoner of Mao* mentions lens making on a primitive scale. Shortly after his arrest in December, 1957, while he was being held in a makeshift prison just outside Beijing, the factory next door housing juvenile delinquents was involved in grinding lenses from glass recycled from Coca Cola bottles left by the Americans in 1949! At the time of his writing in the early 1970s, he still owned a pair of eye glasses with one lens of the light green colour used in Coke bottles.

The original Da Lai 35mm rangefinder camera used lens elements from a

Zorki camera lens. The same thing has been said about the first Shanghai 58-I cameras, though this has not been confirmed by the Shanghai Camera Factory.

The list of cameras copied by the Chinese is a long one. The Da Lai 35mm rangefinder was officially copied from the Zorki of 1955, though the designer himself admits the true model was a Leica IIIb. The Chinese also made the Changle, a copy of the Russian Lubitel, originally a copy of the Voigtlander Brilliant, complete with a swing away door for the storage of two filters. The Zi Jin Shan copied the Zenit SLR of 1956. The Hua Shan and Chiang Jiang copied the Smena. In Nanjing, one factory even copied the Russian FED-2 camera.

European Influence

The influence of the European Communists came to an end in the early 1960s, with the broadening differences between China and the governments of its Brothers. Finally, in 1963, Mao sent all of the technicians home, and broke completely with Eastern Europe. The departing advisers were forced to leave behind tooling and even whole factories built in co-operation with the Chinese.

The factories making cameras carried on until they had exhausted their stocks of imported lenses and shutters. When the last shutter and lens were used, these factories closed down or turned to other business.

Today, the secondhand store shelves show quite a variety of cameras from this period of co-operation: Opema, Belmira, Zenit, Leningrad, Zorki, FED, Reflekta, Start, Contax S, Moscow, Werra, Smena, Symbol, and Krystal cameras regularly make their way onto the shelves. Some, like the Zenit-4, and the Krystal are quite rare in the West.

It isn't too hard to put together a collection of FED cameras, or find most of the different models of Zorki made since 1949, including the Olympic Zorki-5, commemorating the Moscow Olympics of 1980.

Accessory lenses are harder to find, but they do exist. The f=133mm(!) 1:2.8 TDIR-11 and the f=35mm 1:2.8 MIR-1 both won the Grande Prix in Brussels in 1958, or at least that is what is proclaimed on their lens barrels. These two lenses can be used on the Zi Jin Shan camera, and are sometimes found.

The only Russian lenses known to have been copied by the Chinese are the 500mm and 1000mm mirror lenses, which are still sold new. The 1000mm lens fetches more than 1800 US$, but not from me!

Chinese camera collectors

CAMERA COLLECTING IS not the rage in China. It took almost three years and many miles of travel before I met a bonafide collector.

Every secondhand store I went into, I would ask if there were any other camera collectors who were regular customers. Only once did a clerk respond that there was a man who stopped by every once in a while, and that he bought old cameras. I never did learn his name, and he never looked me up, though I left my calling card at the shop for the clerk to give to him.

TIANJIN

It wasn't until I was invited to Tianjin, to the Foreign Languages Institute there to give a lecture on The History of Photography, and How to Collect Cameras, that I met my first collector face to face.

My invitation was offered by the Tianjin Branch of the Chinese Photographers' Association. My lecture had already been cancelled once, and I was running out of time before I was to leave China for a summer holiday.

When Xiao Jia and I finally did arrive, we were met at the station by the head of the Tianjin branch of the Chinese Photographers' Association, and his assistant. The sponsor from the Foreign Language Institute was also there. As it turned out, Mr. Chen from the Institute had been collecting cameras for more than ten years, and was very excited to meet me.

Chen is 33 years old, and works in the audio visual section of the Foreign Languages Institute. His office is in the control room of the school studio, where teaching videos are made. It is also his job to copy video tapes for distribution to other schools. He has very busy times, but also has lots of times when he can pretty much do as he pleases.

During the Cultural Revolution, for all intents and purposes, the schools in China closed, and young Chen stayed home just like millions of other Chinese school-age children.

He was given a lens from an 8mm movie camera, and succeeded in building his own 35mm camera from scratch. This camera still works, and is one of the proudest pieces in his collection.

He is on good terms with the manager of one of the largest secondhand stores in Tianjin. Most of his recent cameras have come from this store, but there is one small problem. The manager is himself a collector, and only passes on his duplicates and cameras in which he is not interested.

Since all secondhand stores are owned by the state, this manager is able to support his collecting habit without touching his salary. He does it like this.

When a camera comes in to which he takes a liking, he buys it outright, using store funds and rather than put it on sale, at a profit for the store, he keeps it. His collection is on display in the store, and represents his efforts over the last few years. Until recently, Mr. Chen was able to have first chance at all the Chinese cameras which came in over the counter of this store. He has been able to collect several very rare and interesting cameras in this way.

Chen is interested in quality European cameras, and has a collection amounting to about thirty cameras from the 1930s and 1940s. One of the most beautiful cameras in his collection is a Zeiss Tropen Adoro in mint condition. What makes this camera especially nice is the *For China* marking on the inside of the body. He picked this camera up for 37 RMB yuan several years ago.

Like collectors everywhere, Chen finds cameras in the oddest places. One morning while on his way to work, he noticed an old man going through some rubbish. He stopped and watched as the old man picked up a junk camera. Mr. Chen ended up buying the camera, a Xing Fu-2, for 1 RMB yuan.

Chen isn't too keen to let other people know that he collects cameras. He is afraid of having his apartment robbed. For this reason, he stores his cameras in several different places. Some are under his bed, others are in boxes in the back of a cupboard. Many of his best cameras are stored at his parents' house.

Another reason Chen is closed mouth about his collecting, concerns money. He is afraid the price of old cameras will go up if it becomes too widely known that there is someone who actually wants to buy them.

As it is now, some of the rarest Chinese cameras don't show up on the secondhand store shelves because the owners feel they can't get anything for them, and the store managers feel that they can't make enough money on them, when and if they do sell.

For several years, Chen has wanted to write about the history of camera production in China, but has had a very hard time getting information. His inquiries to the Ministry of Light Industry, in charge of camera production on a national level, have all gone unanswered, and he doesn't have the time or resources to travel to gather the information at the different sources. He enjoys his collecting, and his wife doesn't mind, as he only uses his 'bonus' money to indulge his hobby. He did admit though, that he still doesn't have a television, not even a black and white set!

SHANGHAI

Shanghai is full of the same hustle and bustle found in many modern western cities. A New Yorker wouldn't feel too out of place on crowded Nanjing Road. Someone from London might have to look twice to realize that he wasn't home. Even the architecture puts a foreigner at ease, since many of the buildings were built by foreign enterprises during the golden years of the 1920s and 1930s. Shanghai was the financial capital of China during that time. Today, Shanghai people are working to rebuild their city, and once again enter the 20th Century.

Mr. Zhou is 62 years old and retired as a middle school teacher of physics. His father worked for one of the large European companies which had offices in Shanghai. Mr Zhou himself worked for a time for an American company, between the end of the Second World War and the liberation of China in 1949.

I came to know Mr. Zhou when he wrote me a letter, saying that he had read my article in *International Photography.* In his letter he asked me to give him some advice about two cameras he had. He wrote in perfect English, but some of the wording struck me as odd.

After exchanging several letters, I arranged to go to Shanghai to visit him.

He lives with his wife in a portion of a former apartment house. Two rooms and no toilet make up his part. His flat does have cold running water, but as everywhere in China, water must be boiled before drinking.

He was waiting in the street when I arrived. He was very excited. When I asked him how it was that he spoke such good English, he explained that I was the first foreigner he had spoken English with in forty years!

He has been collecting cameras for almost twenty years, and has some very fine examples in his collection. One of the cameras he had originally asked me to help him identify is a mint Ergo, by Zeiss. I also helped him figure out how to use the extinction meter in his perfect Voigtlander Prominent.

The cameras in Mr. Zhou's collection are stored with their lenses removed. Shanghai is rather humid, and the lenses are kept in a dry place to prevent fungus growth.

Being retired, Mr. Zhou's time is pretty much his own. Every day he makes it a ritual to visit the secondhand stores in Shanghai. It takes him all afternoon to do it, but rain or shine, at about 4 o'clock he can be found at the counter of the

Old East Gate secondhand store.

This store is the best place to find collectable cameras, so Mr. Zhou tells me. The prices are higher than in other stores, but the selection is better.

He also explained to me that collectable cameras are in ever shorter supply. In the early 1970s Leica IIIf cameras were selling for 300 RMB yuan. French stereo cameras of the 1920s and 1930s were going for 50 RMB yuan. Up until 1984, the store shelves had quite an array of interesting cameras.

At that point, buyers from Japan and Hong Kong were making killings, buying at low prices, and using money obtained at better than official exchange rates, by way of the black market. All that has changed now. Mr. Zhou makes his daily rounds, and seldom comes up with a find.

Like Mr. Chen in Tianjin, Zhou ignored Chinese cameras for the best part of his collecting career. Even though he used a Zi Jin Shan SLR for taking pictures, he didn't like its quality, and sold it. Since the falling off of the numbers of foreign cameras in secondhand stores, he has begun to collect Chinese cameras.

His son is trying to go to the United States to study, and Mr. Zhou was very interested when I explained that if he gave his son a couple of his better cameras, they might easily be turned into financial support. For now, however, he is content to take them out from time to time, and look them over, just like any collector anywhere.

BEIJING

Xiao Liu is only 24 years old, and has a college degree. He works for a camera factory, and has been interested in collecting cameras for only a short time.

Unlike Zhou and Chen, he doesn't use the secondhand store system for his collecting. He counts on his network of friends and associates for leads to cameras in private hands.

Liu already has a theme in his collecting. He wants to collect only Chinese cameras, and then only the most rare cameras, or ones which were made at his factory. He has had very good luck in a relatively short time. Several of the hard to find cameras in this book were photographed from Xiao Liu's collection. He is well on the way to having a really first rate collection. If he continues he may have the best collection of rare Chinese cameras in the world.

He has also discovered that collecting cameras can present problems. Some of his friends are disappointed when they learn that Xiao Liu has paid them only a small percentage of the resale value of their camera. Anywhere else in the world, this might be understood. In China, however, Xiao Liu runs the risk of being denounced as a 'profiteer', or worse, a dreaded capitalist!

CHINESE CAMERA FACTORIES

Beijing
Shanghai
Nanjing
Tianjin

The Da Lai twin lens reflex, made as a prototype by the Beijing factory shortly before it was nationalised.

Beijing camera factory

LATE IN JANUARY, 1988 I had my first chance to visit the Beijing Camera Factory, makers of the Great Wall DF-3 120 SLR. The factory itself isn't too far from my apartment, in the north western suburbs of Beijing. The address on the instruction books enclosed with new cameras reads, *Beijing Camera Factory, near the Big Bell Temple.* In 1987 when I had tried to track it down using my poor Chinese language skills, I had been sent to a small shop selling Great Wall cameras and fishing equipment.

The factory buildings themselves are not out of the ordinary, normal grey-painted brick, devoid of any decoration or embellishment. Inside, in the third floor meeting room, one wall is filled by a large panel displaying a disassembled 35mm camera. It is a Konica, with scale focussing, and built-in flash. The display is rather nicely done, and represents a joint venture with the Konica company of Japan.

The story of the Beijing Camera Factory goes back to the days before 'liberation'. (Officially, 1st October, 1949. The Chinese use this date as a sort of yardstick in time. Events happened either before liberation or after.) In the late 1940s, after the defeat of the Japanese, Beijing was getting itself back on its feet after almost eight years of occupation by the Japanese aggressors (the term used by the Chinese for the occupying Japanese).

The Da Lai Precision Machine Shop

People were thinking of recreation again. Several camera repair shops got together and formed the Da Lai Precision Machine Shop. At first they made tripods, and transits used for surveying.

With the coming of the communist government after 1949, the company, owned by private individuals, was forced to take on the state as a partner as part of the nationalization of private industry. Sometime in 1955 or 1956, the company decided to try its hand at camera making. Because of their co-

The Chang Hong I (left), compared to the Ricohflex VIIS (right), shows its Japanese origins.

operation at that time with the Russians, they decided to copy the Zorki rangefinder camera.

Only twelve Da Lai cameras were made, each one hand-built. No lenses were made for them. However, the metal components of the lens mounts were made in the factory, using only Russian lens elements, intended for the Zorki. The company announced its success on 4th August 1956 with articles appearing in the *Beijing Daily, People's Daily,* and *Workers' Daily.* These articles were accompanied by photographs of workers in the process of putting the cameras together. Sample photos taken with the camera itself were printed, and the quality of the results were praised. That was the last the public heard about the Da Lai camera. Ironically, Da Lai loosely translated means 'very popular'.

One example of the Da Lai camera is known to exist. It is number 100104, and rests in the hands of the Beijing Camera Factory. But I have heard a story of another Da Lai. A student told me that his father, one of the original private owners of the Da Lai Precision Machine Works, had had a Da Lai camera, but it was destroyed by the Red Guards during the Cultural Revolution because it was an example of western ideas.

Given the extreme actions of the Red Guards documented during this period, this story might well be true.

The attempt at making the Da Lai camera came at a very difficult time for the Da Lai Camera Factory. It was being run jointly by the private owners, and the State. Shortly after they began the Da Lai camera experiment, the State took complete control of the factory. The production staff went from less than seventy to more than 500.

The very first thing the new directors did was to change the name of the factory. Hence, the Da Lai Camera Factory became the Beijing Camera Factory.

The first camera made after the government gained control was a twin lens reflex called the Rainbow. It was copied from a Ricoh TLR of the period, and actually was a continuation of the Da Lai TLR prototype, built about the same time as the 35mm Da Lai camera. It used the ruby window system of frame counting. From the information I have, it seems that slightly more than 7,600 Rainbow cameras were made in 1957, the only year of production.

I have found a reference to a May First camera in a 1957 edition of *Chinese Photography*. The announcement included a photograph of the camera. It appears that the name was changed to Da Lai, and the numerals 51 placed between the name characters. It looks like the Rainbow camera, and may have been the name used for the TLR just before the factory was nationalized. The name of the camera of course refers to Labour Day, and is celebrated in Communist Countries, as well as around the free world.

The Great Leap Forward

The year 1958 saw the Chinese embark on their ill-fated Great Leap Forward, during which Mao tried his hand at centralizing all production, and collectivizing all agricultural activities. This turned out to be a monumental failure. During this time, the factory produced at least three different cameras.

The first was called the Temple of Heaven, and looked suspiciously like the Rainbow of 1957. It had a coated lens, and was said to have a self timer added. A second TLR, also called the Temple of Heaven, was also made. This one, however, was a copy of the Yashica A and used a crank advance. In total, 271 of the first version were made, while only two of the more advanced model were produced.

In 1961, in the midst of the Great Leap Forward, the factory also made a bakelite 120 camera called Leap Forward or Yue Jin in Chinese Pinyin. This camera is a direct copy of a Pionyr, made by Dufa, in Czechoslovakia. (See *Abring* 111, page 179, camera No.3104).

The Yue Jin was identical to the Pionyr, and represents another example of the close co-operation between the Chinese and the Eastern Bloc during the late 1950s and early 1960s. More than 1,800 Yue Jin cameras were made by the Beijing camera factory.

The end of the 1960s saw a great struggle in China. 1966 was the beginning of the Cultural Revolution, and the Beijing Camera Factory was to play its part.

Anthony Grey, a British journalist for Reuters looked out his window on the night of 18th August 1967 to see the street filled with a mob of Red Guards. That was to be the beginning of his imprisonment, which lasted 806 days. During this time, he was held captive in his residence, and guarded by Revolutionary Guards of the Beijing Camera Factory! In his book *Hostage in Peking,* (Doubleday and Company Inc., printed in the United States 1971, copyright 1970 by Anthony Grey) Mr Grey describes how he was interrogated, and at one point, he saw his cat Ming Ming hanging dead from his balcony, just above his head.

An official of the factory recounted the same story to me, though with more blame on the cat, saying that the workers killed it because it was making too much noise, and disturbing them.

The Camera Factory was not idle guarding Anthony Grey during this time. They were also producing a spring motordrive rangefinder camera, another copy of a Ricoh model. This camera was to have a long production life, and the last model, the Great Wall SZ-2, was in production up until a few years ago.

The Beijing Camera

At first it was called the Beijing camera though the name 'Red Dawn' as used on a prototype. A few were made with political slogans on them, such as *Serve the People,* and *Long Life to Chairman Mao.* The Beijing name for the camera didn't last very long. The leader of the Beijing government did not allow them to use the name. He figured that people in Shanghai, or other places might be offended, and not buy a camera named after the city. At that time, the name Great Wall was chosen and the Great Wall SZ-1 came into production in the late 1960s. In the mid-1970s, the Great Wall SZ-2 replaced the first model, and had internal design changes. These two cameras are still quite common on the secondhand store shelves, usually non operational.

Also in the early 1970s, the factory tried its hand at several other unsuccessful camera designs. The Great Wall EF-1 was said to have been a Rollei SL66 copy, complete with interchangeable back, and 90mm f1:2.8 lens. Only two of these cameras were made. I was told that sometime in 1987 one of these cameras was stolen from the factory offices, however, I cannot confirm this rumour.

Instruction book for the Beijing SZ-1. This model has 'Serve The People' engraved on the front.

At the same time, the factory was busy making the Great Wall 35 - an exact copy of the Rollei 35 - and the Beijing 35mm SLR. Both cameras were made only as prototypes, and no examples exist outside of the factory. Interestingly, the Beijing 35mm SLR was made in co-operation with the Beijing Glass Research Institute, which, it is said, spent tens of thousands of yuan in making the 50mm 1:1.4 lens used on the prototype.

In 1971, the Great Wall BS-3 35mm rangefinder camera was manufactured. It was another copy taken from Ricoh of Japan. This time, the Chinese chose to copy a camera with trigger advance on the bottom. This camera met with no success, and was produced only in test market numbers.

New Premises, New Products

In 1975 the factory moved from its downtown location to the Northwestern suburbs, behind the Big Bell Temple. With new buildings, and larger area for

The Hong Guang, meaning 'Red Light'. It was one of the practice names used for what finally became the Beijing SZ-1 and ended with the Great Wall SZ-2.

production, the company started to branch out. They began to manufacture microfilming equipment and photo copy machines, which they still produce today.

In 1980, using a Pilot Super camera of the 1930s as a guide, a prototype was made of a simple 120 SLR. After testing, it went into production in 1981.

The Great Wall DF-2 is quite a simple camera. It uses 120 film to produce 6 x 6cm or 6 x 4.5cm negatives, by means of a mask insert, and ruby windows in the back. 35mm size paper-backed black and white film is available and requires a special adaptor to hold the roll in place.

The first Great Wall DF-2 had neither self timer nor flash synch. The later models DF-3 and DF-4 added self timer, and pc flash connection plus side mounted hot shoe.

All Great Wall DF-2, DF-3, and DF-4 cameras have the same manual 90mm f1:3.5 coated lens, all elements move for focussing from infinity down to one meter and a guillotine shutter producing speeds of 1/30, 1/60, 1/125, 1/200 second and B. Cocking the shutter lowers the mirror and releases the double exposure prevention button.

A DF-5 camera was planned and tested. It had a five-element lens with front element focussing. It came at the very end of production, and few were made.

After advancing the film, and checking the appropriate ruby window, you are ready to focus on the dim ground-glass and release the shutter, located on the right side of the camera body. Don't worry about having an exposure meter with you, the camera has a small metal plate just behind the focussing hood with aperture suggestions for different lighting conditions at 1/125 second, with ASA 100 film. Be sure to have a translator available, because it is all in Chinese.

Few accessories are available for the DF series. A set of extension tubes lets you get in extra close. Of course you can mount any Leica screw mount lens, just for fun and go bug hunting. Strange as it may seem, the Great Wall DF-2 lens is available as a manual, medium telephoto in some popular 35mm camera mounts. The cost of the lens with tube and mount is more than half the cost of the new camera! Currently, none of the DF series 120 SLR cameras are in production, though some stock exists in the larger stores, and at the factory.

The top of the line Great Wall DF-4, with really hard leather case sells for about US$40 in the retail camera stores of Beijing, while the prices are a little higher in other cities. The Old Model DF-2, with vinyl case I have seen sell new for US$10, about the same price as they are found used in secondhand stores!

The Hong Qi, or 'Red Flag' in English. It was a direct copy of the Leica M4.

Shanghai camera factory

THE SHANGHAI GENERAL Camera Factory is located in Song Jiang County, about 50 kilometres from Shanghai itself. This factory was formed in 1978, when the Shanghai Camera Factories numbers 1, 2 and 5 moved out from the city to this countryside location. The factory has 130,000 square meters of manufacturing area, with a like amount of space as housing for a portion of its workers. Those who don't live at the factory ride one hour each way on a company-provided bus.

Currently, three kinds of 35mm SLRs are being produced at the factory: the DF-104, DF-102, and DF ETM, all based on Minolta cameras. When asked why Minolta was chosen, factory officials responded that directors and engineers of the factory had looked at many different kinds of cameras, and found that the Minolta was the easiest to copy, given the tooling and materials available.

Production of 120 rollfilm cameras is down to almost zero since the end of 1986 because of the influx of 35mm minilabs. Rollfilm cameras are considered black and white cameras; that is, they are for use with black and white film only. The Chinese population today has easy access to 35mm cameras and both domestic and imported colour film.

One of the most interesting cameras made at this factory is the Red Flag 20, a copy of the Leica M4. It was made on the orders of Chiang Ching, the last wife of Mao Tze Dong. During the Cultural Revolution of the late 1960s and early 1970s (officially 1966-76, also known as the 'ten years of unrest', in Chinese). At that time, Chinese firms were trying to show the outside world that they could produce first class quality goods. Camera factories were no exception.

Reverse engineering was used to copy the Leica M4, and the result was a limited success. Less than 200 cameras are said to have been made. Even fewer of the 35mm f/1.4 and 90mm f/2 auxiliary lenses were produced. The cost of the camera to produce was in the tens of thousands of RMB yuan. The factory sold what it could to newspapers, and official government agencies. Some others are said to have been given to heads of state from visiting nations. Some

A Shanghai 58-II, fitted with the Harbin Reflex Viewer and 90mm f/4 lens. The Harbin device was made in 1966, in very small quantities.

of these cameras have recently been uncovered, and have made their way into the collector's market. Production officially ended in 1976, but some cameras and lenses were put together in 1977 and their serial numbers bear this out.

A First Prototype

In 1957 the first prototype of the Shanghai 58-I camera was made. Production started in 1958, and this is where the camera gets its model designation. It is, screw for screw, a copy of a Leica IIIb, and even though the factory indicates it is a copy of a Russian Zorki, there is little to show this in the camera itself.

The 58-I proved to have some problems, not the least of which was a temperamental shutter, and high production costs. It stayed in production for less than a year, with between 1,000 and 2,000 cameras having been made. (Serial numbers have not been seen higher than 5802XXX) The year 1959 saw the introduction of the new and improved version. The Shanghai 58-II came on the market for 200 RMB yuan, and was to last through several mechanical variations until 1963. Though both the 58-I and 58-II used the M39-1 screw mount, no other lenses were made for use on these cameras. (One exception, however, is the Harbin close-up device, with 90mm lens.)

The Shanghai Camera Factory's line of twin lens reflexes began in 1959, at about the same time as the 58-II camera was being produced. Called the 58-III in the early stages of development, it was marketed as the Shanghai. Based on the Rolleiflex, it even has some parts that are interchangeable.

The Shanghai TLR has an f/2.8, 75mm viewing lens labelled only with the company logo and a serial number. The taking lens is an f/3.5, 75mm labelled with the Shanghai logo, and a completely different serial number from the viewing lens. It also has some other markings on it. The series S13-111-1 is in front of the serial number. The camera serial number is located on top of the body casting, just above the name plate. All Shanghai TLR's numbers begin 63XXXXX.

How the Shanghai 58-II was announced. This was a new and improved version of the Shanghai 58-I that had suffered from a rather temperamental shutter. The inspiration was the Leica IIIb.

The fourth version of the Shanghai 58-II, fitted with a Russian Jupiter-II 135mm telephoto lens.

In 1964, when it was decided to enter the export market, the Seagull name was chosen as the registered trade mark of the Shanghai Camera Factory, and all cameras then in production had their names changed to reflect this.

Therefore the Shanghai TLR became the Seagull-4 TLR. No physical changes were made in the camera, only the names are different. A new serial number configuration was also used, serial numbers for the Seagull-4 now began 4-63XXXXX, to indicate the model.

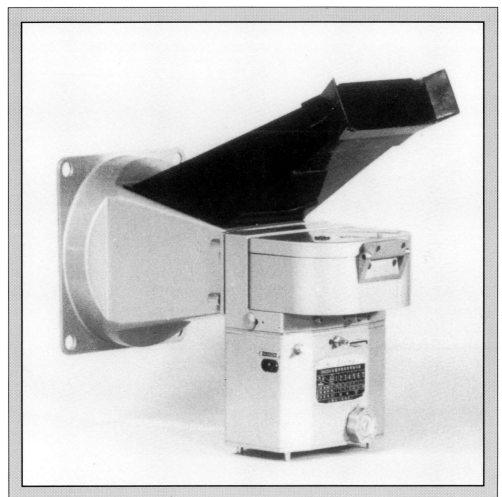

Special 24 x 24mm Recording Camera, made by the Shanghai No.3 factory about 1972.

Since both the Shanghai TLR and the Seagull-4 have automatic film advance, (though the shutter isn't connected, and must be reset manually), they lack the ruby windows found on most Chinese 120 cameras. The frame number appears in the centre of a window in the film advance knob. Later, a film advance crank was added and the model designation changed to 4A. The depth of field scale for both the Shanghai and Seagull-4 is found in a clear window in the focussing knob. The latest version of these cameras is called the 4A-103. It incorporates

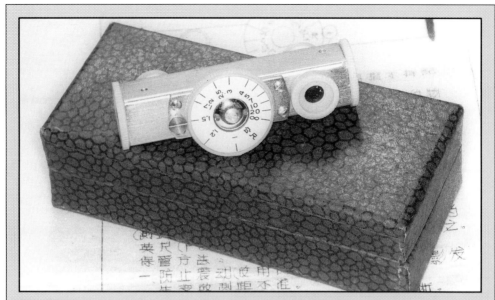

This accessory rangefinder was made by the Clock and Watch department of a Shanghai department store, probably in the late 1960s.

a single action focussing hood. A 4A-1 with old style focussing hood, a fresnel focussing screen, and a four element taking lens instead of the three element Cooke type lens used on all other Seagull TLRs was produced. It was made for the up scale market, and had limited success.

A Different Market

The 4B camera was designed, on the other hand, to sell on the down scale market. It uses ruby windows, and the three element Cooke type lens of the 4A. The good part of this is that with two ruby windows, you can choose between 6 x 6cm, or 6 x 4.5cm negative formats. The 4B comes with a slip-in metal mask for the 6 x 4.5cm negative size. The 4B-1 has ruby windows, and the same three element lens as the 4A-103 and 4B, but comes with an accessory shoe and fresnel focussing screen. All these TLRs have in common a manually set between-the-lens shutter with speeds of 1 to 1/300 second and bulb.

The first folding 120 roll film camera made in China was the Shanghai 201, made in 1958. This simple viewfinder camera had a three element lens, and ruby window frame counting system for 12 exposures 6 x 6cm, and 16 exposures 6 x 4.5cm (with built in mask). Shortly after production began, a self timer and PC flash synch were added, and the model designation was changed to Shanghai 202. The 202 camera was made until 1963, and exists with two styles of script, the line script being the last year's design.

A close look at any one of these three cameras shows their origins quite plainly. They are copied from the simple Agfa Isolette cameras of the period.

The Seagull 203 rangefinder rollfilm camera began its life, as did many of the cameras, from this factory. It was called a Shanghai 203, and followed the 201 and 202 cameras design. The name was quickly changed, however, and the Seagull 203 came on the market in 1964.

Mamiya and Zeiss

It is a folding 120 camera with a coupled rangefinder. The story is that this camera is a mixture of Mamiya and Zeiss, but one couldn't tell by looking at it. It also uses the ruby window system of frame counting, with the same built-in masks for 6 x 4.5cm as the 201 and 202 cameras. These masks take the form of hinged plates, pinned into each film well. Since they are a part of the camera, they can never be lost, as can the metal inserts used on the TLRs. Originally, the Shanghai 203 and subsequently the Seagull 203 used a metal advance lever, and had an exposure guide built into the top plate. A prototype Seagull 203-3 was made eliminating the exposure guide, but was never produced. The Seagull 203 eventually lost its metal advance lever and exposure guide, but no model designation change was made.

The final cameras produced were all in black, using black plastic for the entire top plate, and some were marked Seagull 203-H, the 'H' being the initial for the Pinyin spelling of the Chinese word for black.

Though production has stopped, a few of these black cameras can still be found on the shelves of out of the way camera stores, being sold at a discount.

Several prototype cameras are on display at the factory. Among them is a very interesting 120 degree wideangle camera, for 6 x 9cm exposures on 120 rollfilm, called the Seagull Super Wide Angle Camera, made in 1973. The lens was designed in the factory, and was a 30mm f/8. It covered the 6 x 9cm format from corner to corner, or so I was told.

A copy of the Polaroid 185 was made in 1969, and has an unusual name. It is called the Serve The People 207. The phrase *Serve The People* was made popular by Chairman Mao during the Cultural Revolution (1966-1976). The phrase is inscribed in red on the front of the viewfinder housing, and is actually copied from Mao's own handwriting! The camera was, however, a total failure. Though it functioned well, the film produced by the Shanghai Film Factory was of very poor quality. Less than 100 of these cameras were made.

It is interesting to note that the Shanghai Factory was not the only one putting slogans onto camera bodies. The Beijing Camera Factory also produced 'politicized' models during the same period, including one with *Long Live Chairman Mao* inscribed on it.

With neither viewing system, nor accessory shoe for attaching an auxiliary finder, the DF-AB and DF-C special purpose cameras use a body based on the Red Flag 20. The lenses used were 58mm normal lenses, like on the DF-102 35mm SLR cameras, but were attached using a screw mounting flange. The DF-C has only bulb shutter setting, while the DF-AB has a range of shutter speeds from 1 to 1/60 second. They are used for photographing static set ups, such as CRTs. They were also available for use as microscope cameras, without lenses.

Some of these cameras are still being used in labs in hospitals, and are still sent to the Shanghai Factory authorized repair station from time to time.

The Shanghai General Camera Factory is the largest camera manufacturer in China. It exports its products to many foreign countries, and enjoys a good reputation for quality.

Inside and outside first and fourth versions (shown left and right respectively), of the Shanghai 58-II, differences in manufacture can be seen.

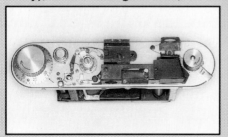

Nanjing motion picture equipment factory

AT ABOUT THE same time that the Shanghai Camera Factory was making the 58-II rangefinder camera, the Nanjing Motion Picture Equipment Factory was deciding to enter the marketplace with a still camera of its own.

This factory, located at the foot of the Purple Mountains in the suburbs of Nanjing, was already making motion picture cameras and projectors. They were doing quite a good business providing portable generator-powered 16mm projectors (based on a Russian design) for the government. These were used to bring 'enlightenment' to the countryside. Teams of propaganda specialists showed films of the liberation of China to the illiterate peasants in the remotest parts of the Chinese territories. At the same time the factory was also making a copy of the 35mm Arriflex motion picture camera, for use in filming documentaries. They had the knowhow and the tools to produce first-rate motion picture equipment and they wanted to try their hand at a 35mm still camera.

When the idea first came up to produce a 35mm SLR, a design team studied several different cameras, in order to decide which camera would be the best one to copy. As with the Leica IIIb copy from Shanghai, this factory didn't think of making their own camera, but of copying another already successful model.

Leica, Werra or Zenit?

Three cameras were considered: first, the Leica IIIc; second an East German Werra, notable for its odd around-the-lens shutter cocking/film advance system; and third, the one ultimately chosen for copying - the Russian Zenit SLR.

Examples were purchased of each camera, and disassembled. The first two choices were quickly abandoned as being too complicated for economical production, in addition to presenting direct competition to the Shanghai 58-II.

The Zenit SLR, however, was relatively simple to produce and offered the advantage of through-the-lens viewing. Taking its name from the scenic location of the factory, production of the Zi Jin Shan SLR began in earnest in 1959.

The Zi Jin Shan 35mm single lens reflex that was a copy of the Russian Zenit, seen here fitted with a 35mm Russian wideangle lens.

(Actually, the same name was used for a 120 rollfilm twin lens reflex produced at the same time, in the same factory. The TLR, a Rolleicord copy, sold for between 300 and 400 Yuan, and was equipped with a three element Cooke type lens.)

The Zi Jin Shan came supplied with a coated four element Tessar type lens, in a 39mm screw thread mount and a maximum aperture of f/3.5. At the very end of production, about thirty cameras were provided with a f/2.8 lens. No other lenses were made for this camera, though Russian tele and wideangle lenses, made to fit the Zenit SLR, could be purchased and worked fine.

The Purple Mountain SLR cost a healthy 200 Yuan, about four months pay for a factory worker back in those days.

One of the curious features of this camera is its lack of instant return mirror. Not only does the mirror not come down immediately after the shutter is fired, it doesn't even come down upon advancing to the next frame. Located to the left of the lens, and looking every bit like a self timer lever is the means of lowering the mirror!

The factory design team originally had plans for three models of the camera. The second model would have had an instant return mirror, X type flash synch, and a self timer. The third was intended to have a new type bayonet lens mount, and a 35-70mm zoom lens.

All of these well thought out plans were scrapped for a very interesting reason. It seems that the manufacture of motion picture equipment falls under the direction of the Ministry of Culture, whilst the manufacture of still cameras is controlled by the Ministry of Light Industry. In 1961, the Nanjing Motion Picture Equipment Factory was ordered to stop producing both types of Purple Mountain still cameras. The tools, drawings, and some forty workers were sent into the Jiangsu Province countryside to set up a new factory to continue making the SLR. Without the support of the main factory, the new venture was doomed to failure. Not a single camera was made at the new factory.

The tools and drawings have since been lost, and nothing was ever heard about the Purple Mountain camera again. (The only other connection the Nanjing factory had with the production of a still camera up until the present, was when it 'loaned' skilled workers to the Shanghai camera factory in 1963 in order to help them out with their Seagull series cameras).

In the three years of its production, less than 1,000 SLRs were made. An even smaller quantity of the Zi Jin Shan TLR were made. Most of the cameras were sold in the Nanjing area, but some were shipped to the far corners of China. None were known to have been exported.

Dating of the Purple Mountain SLR is actually quite easy. The serial number is found on the lens, not the camera body. The first two digits are the year of production, the following numbers were consecutive, with No.100 being the first camera.

Back In Business

It seems ironic, but now after nearly twenty-five years, the Nanjing Motion Picture Equipment Factory is again producing a 35mm still camera. A compact 35mm RFR camera called the Sanyou (meaning three friends: the photographer, the film, and the camera) is being made for the local market. It fills an important role in providing China with a 'home' made 35mm camera of reasonable price and quality, offering an alternative to the Japanese cameras on the market.

Since it can be purchased with local currency, and does not require foreign exchange, the production of this camera is actually encouraged by the government.

Two views of the July First camera, bearing a strong likeness to the Japanese Mamiya Six, right down to an unusual focal plane focussing mechanism.

Tianjin camera factory

UNLIKE THE BEIJING Camera Factory, located in the far north-western suburbs of the capitol, or the Shanghai Camera Factory, located 50 kilometres outside Shanghai itself, the Tianjin General Camera Factory is situated on a quiet tree-lined urban street. The neighbourhood is located in what was the English concession area of the 1930s when Tianjin, like several other Chinese cities, was home to the Russians, Japanese, French, British, and Germans. These ex-patriots had their own communities, and brought with them their own architecture and landscaping ideas.

The offices of the Tianjin General Camera Factory are housed in what used to be a fine old private home, obviously once the residence of a wealthy foreign merchant or factory owner.

Across New China Street from the administrative offices, current camera production is carried on in a nondescript beige brick building. It wasn't always like this.

In the early 1950s Tianjin had quite a number of workshops producing wooden view cameras for use in Chinese photo studios. Most of these shops had craftsman who worked on a camera from start to finish. Many of the cameras were made of wood imported from the Philipines, and they were really works of art. One example which bears the maker's address as, *'a small lane near the Peoples' Theatre'* has all the screw heads aligned, and came with a companion 120 rollfilm back made entirely of wood.

Eighteen of these workshops joined together and formed the Tianjin Camera Factory in 1956.

The First Camera

The Tianjin Camera Factory is officially recognized by the Chinese Government as having produced the first modern camera in China, after liberation (1st October 1949).

The Japanese Mamiya 6 was faithfully copied by the Tianjin factory to produce the July First camera. This is officially recognised as the first production camera made in China after 'Liberation'.

The July First camera (named in honour of the day in 1921 when the Chinese Communist Party was founded) is a direct copy of the early Mamiya Six 120 rollfilm folding rangefinder cameras, even down to using the unusual moveable focal plane system for focussing. First produced in late 1956, two of these cameras were sent to Egypt as part of an aid package when the Egyptians were fighting the British. The rest of the production stayed in Tianjin, and were used by factory employees.

Eventually, they slipped away, and all but two have disappeared. One of these was loaned to the Ministry of Light Industry for use in a display of manufacturing history which took place in Hangzhou in 1987. There is some concern, as this camera has not yet been returned, leaving the factory with only one example of the July First camera.

Complicated Design

Production stopped after about forty cameras had been made. It seems that the shutter was just too complicated to make. It contained over 170 small precision parts, and the factory didn't have the means to continue producing it.

Looking back, the management now realizes that it made the wrong choice in copying the Mamiya

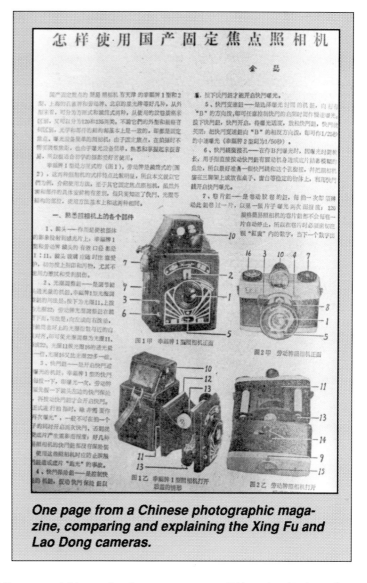

One page from a Chinese photographic magazine, comparing and explaining the Xing Fu and Lao Dong cameras.

Six camera. They feel they would have had more success if they had taken the same path as the Shanghai Camera Factory, and chosen the Leica camera to copy.

In 1957, after production had stopped on the July First, it was decided to make a much simpler camera. The Altissa 120 rollfilm box camera from Eho-Altissa in Dresden was chosen because of its simple design. (Some people at the

51

The Altissa, a simple rollfilm camera from East Germany that was the model for the Chinese Xing Fu. Poor sales forced production of the camera to stop in 1962.

factory insist that a Japanese camera was used as a model, but since the Xing Fu camera bears such a resemblance to the Altissa I feel they must be misre-membering).

With a very simple shutter design and fixed focus lens the Xing Fu was a relative success on the commercial market. About 70,000 Xing Fu cameras were made. Unfortunately, few survive because of their less than robust con-struction quality. The Chinese also consider it to be of no value at all, and are just as likely to throw it in the dustbin when they do their spring cleaning, as to keep it. (A Chinese camera collector friend actually picked up a Xing Fu 2 from a garbage picker for one yuan!). Production of the Xing Fu camera stopped in 1962, the reason given being its poor sales. An effort was made to bring out a new and improved model, the Xing Fu 2, but its quality compared to the original was much poorer, and it quickly failed.

An Entirely Chinese Design

During a meeting at Zhejiang University in 1958, a plan was discussed concerning the production of a 35mm single lens reflex camera of superior quality. A design team was formed, the result of which turned out to be the Chenguang SLR.

From when it was first made in 1959 until work was stopped in 1964, only about 170 Chenguang (meaning Dawn) cameras were made. It was the only camera of that period which was entirely of Chinese design. Variations in style were tried, and at least one Chenguang had a light metering cell showing on the front of its pentaprism, though it quite possibly was not functional, and only used for promotional purposes.

Four normal lenses of different apertures were tested, 1:3.5, 1:2.8, 1:2.0, and 1:1.7, all were 50mm focal length, and all sported the same strange 45mm screw mount. No wideangle or telephoto lenses were made.

All of the Chenguang SLRs were sold or distributed either inside the Tianjin Camera Factory, or Zhejiang University.

As with the Shanghai brand at the Shanghai Camera Factory, an interest in the export market killed the Chenguang name.

In 1964, the factory chose the Yashica Minister D camera to copy, without its built-in light meter. In 1965 full scale production began. This proved to be a wise choice, and with only a few cosmetic changes, this robust 35mm rangefinder camera, called the Eastar in English (though a better translation would be The East) is still in production today.

In the late 1970s, using the design made popular by the Seagull 4B camera, the factory began producing the Eastar TLR. Production lasted only four years, and the camera was not an economic success.

In 1984 a production line was imported from Hong Kong. Now the EF-35 camera is being made using this production line. Like its ancestor the Xing Fu, it is a fixed focus camera.

The Tianjin Camera Factory is still going strong today, and the staff expect to keep producing cameras into the next century.

CHINESE CAMERA MODELS

Beijing
Shanghai
Nanjing
Tianjin
Others

Cameras from Beijing

BEIJING SZ-1

Da Lai (Popular)

Front, back and top... the Da Lai 135. Only one is now known to exist.

Factory: Da Lai Camera Factory, Beijing.

Camera Type: Split image rangefinder with interchangeable lens, using 135 film. Bottom loading.

Taking Lens: Coated f=50mm, 1:3.5, three elements in three groups, collapsible tube with M39-1 screw thread. The lens elements are said to come from the Zorki camera, while all the mounting was hand-made at the Da Lai factory.

Viewing Lens: Separate viewing and focussing windows, as in Leica IIIb, no dioptre adjustment.

Shutter: Cloth focal plane shutter with speeds from 1/20 sec to 1/1000 sec,* including T and B. No slow speeds, no flash synch, no self timer.

Dates of Production: Announced in *People's Daily* on 4th August 1956.

Number Produced: 12

Serial Number Information: Located on the top plate, beginning 1001XX.

Selling Price: Never sold.

Features: Strap lugs on body, three screw accessory shoe, as on Zorki cameras.

Remarks: Camera number 100104, held by the Beijing Camera Factory is the only known example of the Da Lai 135 camera existing today, though rumour has it that one more might be stored away in a former worker's home. The lens shows only focal length and aperture information, no logo or indication of manufacturer appears.

* This camera has a shutter speed dial indicating slow speeds should be found in the shutter speed range, however, no slow speeds exist. Whether slow speeds were intended, and never incorporated, or if the shutter speed setting dial is a replacement, may never be known.

Da Lai (Popular)

The Da Lai twin lens reflex. Note the number 51 incorporated in the logo and standing for 1st. May.

Factory: Da Lai Camera Factory, Beijing.

Camera Type: Twin Lens Reflex.

Taking Lens: Coated f=8cm, 1:3.5, three elements in three groups, gear coupled to the viewing lens for focussing.

Viewing Lens: Coated f=8cm, 1:3.5.

Shutter: Manually set between the lens type with speeds of 1 sec to 1/300 sec plus B. No self timer or flash synch.

Dates of Production: 1957.

Number Produced: ?

Serial Number Information: The serial number is located around the taking lens.

Selling Price: ?

Features: Folding focussing screen magnifier, sports finder incorporated in the viewfinder hood.

Remarks: The Da Lai TLR was made as a prototype just before the Da Lai Factory was nationalised, and became the Beijing Camera Factory. The Da Lai TLR was announced as the May First camera, and did have the numerals 51 on the nameplate. It was actually produced and marketed as the Chang Hong I (Rainbow) soon after, and then with only the addition of a self timer, the Chang Hong II. Finally, the camera saw its last incarnation with the nameplate Tian Tan.

Chang Hong II (Rainbow)

Factory: Beijing Camera Factory, Beijing.

Camera Type: Twin Lens Reflex.

Taking Lens: Coated f=8cm, 1:3.5, three elements in three groups, gear coupled to the viewing lens for focussing.

Viewing Lens: Coated f=8cm, 1:3.5.

Shutter: Manually set between-the-lens type with speeds of 1 sec to 1/300 sec plus B. Self timer and flash synch.

Dates of Production: 1957.

Number Produced: 7,600.*

Serial Number Information: The serial number is located around the taking lens, with another number located on the shutter at the bottom.

Selling Price:100 RMB yuan.

Features: Folding focussing screen magnifier, and a sports finder are incorporated in the viewfinder hood.

The Chang Hong II. How the Da Lai twin lens reflex changed when the Da Lai factory was nationalised.

Remarks: The Chang Hong II camera is what became of the Da Lai TLR after the Da Lai Camera Factory was nationalised. It differs from the Chang Hong I by the addition of a self timer.

* This number includes both Chang Hong I and Chang Hong II production figures.

Xing Guang (Star Light)

The Xing Guang. The camera pictured shows only f/11 and f/16 marked, although the official announcement indicated f/8 as the maximum aperture.

Factory: Beijing Camera Factory, Beijing.

Camera Type: Simple viewfinder camera.

Taking Lens: Two elements fixed focus from 1.7m to infinity. Three stops - f/8, f/11, and f/16.

Shutter: Between-the-lens with speeds of 1/25 sec and B.

Dates of Production: 1959.

Number Produced: ?

Serial Number Information: No serial number appeared on this camera.

Selling Price: 49 RMB yuan with case.

Features: A frame counter is located on top of the camera, much as the Hua Shan camera, shutter lock, unique plastic screw holds on back.

Remarks: The Starlight camera has a thermoplastic body. Though introduced to the public in 1959, it was never made in large quantities, and all that were made were sold in the Beijing area.

Tian Tan
(Temple of Heaven)

Factory: Beijing Camera Factory, Beijing.

Camera Type: Twin Lens Reflex.

Taking Lens: Coated f=8cm, 1:3.5, three elements in three groups, coupled to the viewing lens for focussing.

Viewing Lens: Coated f=8cm, 1:3.5.

Shutter: Manually set between the lens type with speeds of 1 sec to 1/300 sec plus B. Self timer and flash synch.

Dates of Production: 1959-61.

Number Produced: 273.

Serial Number Information: The serial number is located around the taking lens.

Selling Price: 130 RMB yuan in 1959.

Features: Folding focussing screen magnifier, sports finder incorporated in the viewfinder hood.

Remarks: The Tian Tan camera existed in at least two distinct models. The first was a direct copy of the Ricoh VIIS TLR, with the taking lens geared to the viewing lens. At first, this model sported *Tian Tan* in Chinese characters, then later, the Pinyin spelling. This was a continuation of the Da Lai camera started before the Beijing Camera Factory evolved. The second model was a copy of the Yashica A camera, with lens standard focussing and crank type film advance. Only two prototypes of this second model were made, one of which is still at the factory.

Tian Tan
(Temple of Heaven)

Factory: Beijing Camera Factory, Beijing.

Camera Type: Twin Lens Reflex.

Taking Lens: Coated f=8cm, 1:3.5, three elements in three groups.

Viewing Lens: Coated f=8cm, 1:3.5.

Shutter: Automatically set with film advance between the lens type with speeds of 1 sec to 1/500 sec plus B. Self timer and flash synch.

Dates of Production: 1961.

Number Produced: 2.

Serial Number Information: The serial number is located around the viewing lens.

Selling Price: Never sold.

Features: Folding focussing screen magnifier, sports finder incorporated in the viewfinder hood.

The second model of the Tian Tan twin lens reflex. Only two prototypes were made before the factory gave up the project.

Remarks: The Tian Tan, the second model, is a copy of the Yashica A camera, with lens standard focussing, and crank type film advance. Only two prototypes were made before the project was given up.

Yuejin (Great Leap)

Two of a kind. Left, the Pionyr from Dufa in Prague, compared with the Yuejin (right).

Factory: Beijing Camera Factory, Beijing.

Camera Type: Simple viewfinder camera.

Taking Lens: Uncoated two elements scale focussing at 1m, 1.5m, 2.5m and infinity, by use of detents in the lens mount. Choice of two apertures, marked 1 (f/8) and 2 (f/11).

Viewing Lens: Optical glass direct vision viewfinder.

Shutter: Between-the-lens type, with I and B settings, marked M (1/25 sec) and T (B).

Dates of Production: 1961.

Number Produced: 1,800.

Serial Number Information: No serial number appeared on this camera.

Selling Price: 40 RMB yuan.

Features: Choice of two apertures, marked 1 and 2. Shutter lock. Helical focussing mount with four-zone focussing positions.

Remarks: The Yuejin camera is another example of the co-operation between the Chinese and their Eastern Bloc Socialist friends. The factory in Beijing was set up by the Czechs, and in the early 1960s, when they were asked to leave by the Chinese, the factory production became entirely Chinese for the home market. The camera itself is marked *Beijing Product* in Chinese Pinyin on the front of the lens housing. This camera is the same in every respect as the Fit-II camera from Dufa, in Prague.

EF-1

The EF-1. Using the Rollei SL 66 as a starting point, the camera was made to compete with the Shanghai factory's Dong Feng.

Factory: Beijing Camera Factory, Beijing.

Camera Type: 120 SLR, with interchangeable lenses, and interchangeable backs.

Taking Lens: Coated f=90mm 1:2.8, focussing from 1m to infinity.

Viewing Lens: Removable waist-level finder, with interchangeable focussing screens, and built-in focussing magnifier.

Shutter: Cloth focal plane shutter with speeds of 1 sec to 1/500 sec. X and M synch, no self timer.

Dates of Production:1970.

Number Produced: 2.

Serial Number Information: The serial number appears around the lens, while the body has no number of its own.

Selling Price: Never sold.

Features: Interchangeable finders and backs, and lenses, though none were ever produced.

Remarks: This camera was an attempt to compete with the Dong Feng camera made by the Shanghai Camera Factory. The Beijing Camera Factory chose to use the Rollei SL 66 camera as its starting point.* As with many of the German cameras copied, the EF-1 proved too difficult and costly to manufacture.

* The factory insists that the SL 66 was the starting point for their creation, though the end result bears little resemblance to the Rollei.

Beijing

Front and back of the Beijing 35mm single lens reflex. Note the serial number 10,001 and 'Beijing Optical Glass Research Institute' in Chinese characters.

Factory: Beijing Camera Factory, Beijing.

Camera Type: 35mm SLR, with interchangeable lenses.

Taking Lens: Coated f=50mm. 1:1.4 focussing from 0.4m to infinity.

Viewing Lens: Pentaprism TTL viewing, no incorporated light meter.

Shutter: Cloth focal plane shutter with speeds from 1 sec to 1/1000 sec plus B.

Dates of Production: 1964.

Number Produced: 2.

Serial Number Information: The lens serial number appears around the lens bezel, the body number is on the back of the top plate.

Selling Price: Never sold.

Features: M and X type synch, mirror lock up. No accessory shoe. Breech lock type lens mount, similar to, but not interchangeable with, Canon. No accessory lenses were ever made.

Remarks: The Beijing SLR camera was an attempt to enter the SLR market with a home product. One of the big drawbacks was the cost of research. It is said the lens alone cost tens of thousands of yuan to perfect. The camera was made in co-operation with the Beijing Optical Glass Research Institute, whose name appears on the back of the top plate.

Great Wall BS-3

The Great Wall BS-3. A 35mm rangefinder camera, made under the influence of Ricoh.

Factory: Beijing Camera Factory, Beijing.

Camera Type: Split image rangefinder with fixed lens.

Taking Lens: Coated f=45mm 1:2.8 focussing from 0.9m to infinity.

Viewing Lens: Combined rangefinder/viewfinder window showing field of view for 45mm lens, bright line parallax correction.

Shutter: Between-the-lens type with speeds of 1 sec to 1/300 sec plus B. Self timer, flash synch.

Dates of Production: 1971.

Number Produced: ?

Serial Number Information: The serial number appears around the lens, with the first two digits giving the year of manufacture.

Selling Price: ?

Features: Bottom-mounted trigger advance, the film rewind is also located on the bottom plate.

Remarks: This is another example of the Beijing Camera Factory copying a Japanese camera, and then failing to market it. The original design came from a Ricoh camera. No information has been found concerning a BS-1 or BS-2 model. BS may stand for the Pinyin spelling of Beijing City *Beijing Shir.*

Beijing SZ-1

The Beijing SZ-1. This model has 'Serve The People' inscribed in Chinese characters on the top plate.

Factory: Beijing Camera Factory, Beijing.

Camera Type: 35mm rangefinder with fixed lens.

Taking Lens: Coated f=45mm. 1:2.8 coupled to rangefinder, focussing from 0.9m to infinity.

Viewing Lens: Split image rangefinder, with field of view for 45mm lens.

Shutter: Between-the-lens type, 1/30 to 1/300 sec plus B. Self timer, PC flash synch.

Dates of Production: 1968-69.

Number Produced: Less than 5,000?

Serial Number Information: Both the lens and the camera body have a serial number. The number on the lens, located on the lens bezel, is preceded by SZ and contains five digits. The body number is located on the back of the top plate, to the right of the viewfinder. It also begins SZ, but has six digits. *Beijing Camera Factory* is written in Chinese above the body number.

Selling Price: 125 RMB yuan?

Features: The Beijing SZ-1 camera is a copy of a Ricoh camera, and has a built-in spring motor advance. About eight frames can be shot before rewinding the motor. The shutter lock, located around the shutter release, is marked S (free) and I (locked).

Remarks: This is another example of a camera which came on the market during the Cultural Revolution. The earliest cameras sported popular political slogans of that era, such as *Serve the People* (reproduced in Mao's handwriting) and *Long live Chairman Mao.* These slogans were written on every possible surface. *Serve the People* can still be seen today in some stores and offices, displayed on the wall in huge characters.

Great Wall 35

Factory: Beijing Camera Factory, Beijing.

Camera Type: Full frame compact 35mm camera with collapsible lens mount.

Taking Lens: Coated f=40mm 1:3.5, scale focussing from 0.9m to infinity.

Viewing Lens: Eye-level optical viewfinder showing field of view for full frame 35mm negative.

Shutter: Between-the-lens type, with speeds of 1 sec to 1/500 sec plus B. No self timer, hot shoe flash synch on base plate.

Dates of Production: 1972.

Number Produced: 5.

Serial Number Information: No serial number appears on this camera.

Selling Price: Never sold.

Features: Wrist strap, exposure guide on top plate.

Remarks: The Great Wall 35 is a complete copy of the very compact Rollei 35 camera of the late 1960s. It was made at a time when the camera factory was trying to impress their government leaders with their skill in camera manufacturing. Of the five cameras produced, only one is known to exist, at the factory.

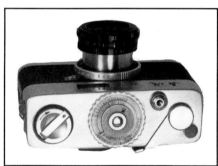

The Great Wall 35, copied directly from the Rollei 35

Great Wall SZ-1

Front and rear views of the Great Wall SZ-1, a continuation of the original Beijing SZ-1.

Factory: Beijing Camera Factory, Beijing.

Camera Type: Rangefinder with fixed lens.

Taking Lens: Coated f=45mm. 1:2.8 coupled to rangefinder, focussing 0.9m to infinity.

Viewing Lens: Split-image rangefinder, with field of view for 45mm lens.

Shutter: Between-the-lens type, 1/30 to 1/300 sec plus B. Self timer, PC flash synch.

Dates of Production: 1969-77.

Number Produced: More than 100,000 were made (including SZ-2).

Serial Number Information: Both the lens and the camera body have a serial number. The number on the lens is

located on the lens bezel, and is preceded by SZ. The body number is located on the back of the top plate, to the right of the viewfinder, the first two digits indicating the year of manufacture. *Made in China* is written in Chinese characters above the body serial number.

Selling Price: 125 RMB yuan?

Features: This camera is a copy of a Ricoh camera, and has a built-in spring motor advance. About eight frames can be shot before rewinding the motor. Shutter lock around the release, marked I (free) and L (locked).

Remarks: The Great Wall SZ-1 camera continued from the Beijing SZ-1 of the early Cultural Revolution. The name was changed to help sell the camera in areas outside of Beijing. It has a reputation as being hard to repair, and easily broken. Numerous complaints led to the improved model SZ-2 in 1979.

Great Wall SZ-2

The Great Wall SZ-2, an improved version of the Great Wall SZ-1

Factory: Beijing Camera Factory, Beijing.

Camera Type: Rangefinder with fixed lens.

Taking Lens: Coated f=45mm. 1:2.8 coupled rangefinder focussing from 0.9m to infinity.

Viewing Lens: Split-image rangefinder with field of view for 45mm lens.

Shutter: Between-the-lens type, 1/30 to 1/300 sec plus B. Self timer, PC flash synch.

Dates of Production: 1976-80.

Number Produced: More than 100,000 were made (including SZ-1).

Serial Number Information: Both lens and the camera body have a serial number. The first two digits do not denote the year of manufacture. *Made in China* in English appears above the body number.

Selling Price: 150 RMB yuan?

Features: The last in the line of Ricoh camera copies containing a built-in spring motor advance. The shutter lock around the release, is marked L (locked) and I (free).

Remarks: At present this camera does not appear new on store shelves, but can be easily purchased secondhand. It has an improved shutter system, and a sturdier spring motor than the Great Wall SZ-1.

Great Wall DF-2

Factory: Beijing Camera Factory, Beijing.

Camera Type: 120 rollfilm SLR.

Taking Lens: Coated f=90mm 1:3.5, focussing from 1m to infinity, in M39-1 screw thread mount.

Viewing Lens: Non interchangeable waist-level viewfinder, with fields for 6 x 4.5cm and full-frame 35mm ruled on ground glass.

Shutter: Metal guillotine type, manually set with speeds of 1/30 sec to 1/200 plus B.

Dates of Production: 1981-85.*

Number Produced: Tens of thousands.*

Serial Number Information: The serial number is located on the inside, printed on paper and glued to the body.

Selling Price: 90 RMB yuan with case.

Features: Folding magnifier in the hood and exposure suggestion table on top. Ruby window frame advance for 12 exposures 6 x 6cm, or 16 exposures 6 x 4.5cm on 120 rollfilm. A special paper-backed 35mm film was sold, along with an adaptor for its use.

The Great Wall DF-2 - the cheapest 120 single lens reflex in the world?

Remarks: The DF-2 is a copy of a very old camera, the Pilot Super of the 1930s made by Kamera Werkstatten AG, which later became VEB Pentacon. The DF-2 could have been improved if, in addition to having copied the Super Pilot's shutter, it had copied its extinction meter too. It must be the cheapest 120 SLR in the world. Now it is easy to find them used for about $10 (US), in Chinese secondhand stores.

***This information includes the DF2, DF3, and DF4 cameras.**

Great Wall DF-3

Factory: Beijing Camera Factory, Beijing.

Camera Type: 120 rollfilm SLR.

Taking Lens: Coated f=90mm 1:3.5, focussing from 1m to infinity, in M39-1 screw thread mount.

Viewing Lens: Non interchangeable waist-level viewfinder, with fields for 6 x 4.5cm and full-frame 35mm ruled on ground glass.

Shutter: Metal guillotine type, manually set with speeds of 1/30 sec to 1/200 plus B. Self timer, no flash synch.

Dates of Production: 1981-85.*

Number Produced: Tens of thousands.*

Serial Number Information: The serial number is located on the inside, printed on paper and glued to the body.

Selling Price: 120 RMB yuan with hard leather case.

Features: Folding magnifier in the hood and exposure suggestion table on top. Ruby window frame advance for 12 exposures 6 x 6cm, or 16 exposures 6 x 4.5cm on 120 rollfilm. A special paper backed 35mm film was sold, along with an adaptor for its use.

Remarks: The DF-3 camera is an improved (by the addition of a self timer!) model of the DF-2, made earlier. A new Great Wall logo was introduced, using more stylized script.

* This information includes DF2, DF3, and DF4 cameras.

Great Wall DF-4

Factory: Beijing Camera Factory, Beijing.

Camera Type: 120 rollfilm SLR.

Taking Lens: Coated f=90mm 1:3.5, focussing from 1m to infinity, in M39-1 screw thread mount.

Viewing Lens: Non interchangeable waist-level viewfinder, with fields for 6 x 4.5cm and full-frame 35mm ruled on ground glass.

Shutter: Metal guillotine type, manually set with speeds of 1/30 sec to 1/200 plus B. Self timer, flash synch, side mounted hot shoe.

Dates of Production: 1981-85.*

Number Produced: Tens of thousands.*

Serial Number Information: The serial number is located on the inside, printed on paper and glued to the body.

Selling Price: 143 RMB yuan with hard leather case.

Features: Folding magnifier in the hood, and exposure suggestion table on top. Ruby window frame advance for 12 exposures 6 x 6cm, or 16 exposures 6 x 4.5cm on 120 rollfilm. A special paper backed 35mm film was sold, along with an adaptor for its use.

The Great Wall DF-4 single lens reflex.

Remarks: The DF-4 camera represents the last of the Great Wall DF cameras. It included flash synch, (a hot shoe mounted on the left side, in addition to PC connection on the front) and the self timer from the DF3. 35mm colour film killed this line of cameras. In the 1980s China was importing Japanese minilabs for the processing of 35mm colour film, and people showed that they would rather have had a simple, plastic 35mm camera, than their medium format cameras of the past.

***This information includes DF2, DF3, and DF4 cameras.**

Cameras from Shanghai

SHANGHAI 58-II (FOURTH VERSION)

Shanghai 58-I

The Shanghai 58-I... China's first successful attempt at copying the Leica IIIb.

Factory: Shanghai Camera Factory, Shanghai.

Camera Type: Split image rangefinder with interchangeable lens, using 135 film. Bottom loading.

Taking Lens: Some coated, some uncoated, f=50mm 1:3.5 three elements in three groups. Collapsible tube with M39-1 screw thread. Focussing from 1.1m to infinity.

Viewing Lens: Separate side-by-side viewing and focussing windows. Dioptre adjustment for focussing window.

Shutter: Cloth focal plane shutter with speeds from 1 sec to 1/1000 sec, including T and B. No flash synch, no self timer.

Dates of Production: 1958.

Number Produced: Less than 2,000

Serial Number Information: On top plate beginning 58XXXXX. No numbers higher than 58002XXX have been seen.

Selling price: 200 RMB yuan, 1958.

Features: Strap lugs on body. Leica type take-up spool retaining shaft. Four-screw accessory shoe, dioptre adjustment.

Remarks: This camera was the first successful Chinese attempt at copying the Leica IIIb camera. It was soon found too costly to make, and was replaced by the Shanghai 58-II, first version. Though it has a removable lens, no accessory lenses were made for it. (A Visoflex type reflex focussing device was made, along with a 90mm close-up lens for use with it. This accessory came from a factory in Harbin, in North-East China).

Shanghai 58-II (1st/2nd versions)

The first version of the Shanghai 58-II. Externally it looks identical to the second version, but minor changes were made inside.

Factory: Shanghai Camera Factory, Shanghai.

Camera Type: Split-image rangefinder with interchangeable lens, using 135 film. Bottom loading.

Taking Lens: Coated f=50mm 1:3.5, three elements in three groups. Collapsible tube with M39-1 screw thread. Focussing from 1.1m to infinity.

Viewing Lens: Single window combining split-image rangefinder and field of view for normal 50mm lens. Dioptre adjustment.

Shutter: Cloth focal plane shutter with speeds from 1 sec to 1/1000 sec, including T and B. PC type flash synch. No self timer.

Dates of Production: 1959?

Number Produced: 2,500.

Serial Number Information: On top plate, beginning 58XXXXX. No numbers higher than 5805XXX have been seen.

Selling Price: 200 RMB yuan, 1959.

Features: Strap lugs on body. Leica type take-up spool retaining shaft. Four-screw accessory shoe.

Remarks: This camera represents the first variation based on the Shanghai 58-I camera of 1958. An attempt was made to reduce production costs by combining the rangefinder and viewfinder windows. Externally this first version 58-II looks exactly like the second version 58-II. Internally, a further attempt at economy on the second version swapped the complicated take-up spool retaining shaft for a simpler one using spring metal fingers.

Shanghai 58-II (3rd version)

The third version of the Shanghai 58-II. Removing strap lugs from the body helped to cut production costs.

Factory: Shanghai Camera Factory, Shanghai.

Camera Type: Split-image rangefinder with interchangeable lens, using 135 film. Bottom loading.

Taking Lens: Coated f=50mm 1:3.5, three elements in three groups. Collapsible tube with M39-1 screw thread. Focussing from 1.1m to infinity.

Viewing Lens: Single window combining split-image rangefinder and field of view for normal 50mm lens. Dioptre adjustment.

Shutter: Cloth focal plane shutter with speeds from 1 sec to 1/1000 sec, including T and B. PC type flash synch. No self timer.

Dates of Production: 1960-61?

Number Produced: 30,000?

Serial Number Information: On top plate, beginning 58XXXXX.

Selling Price: 200 RMB yuan, in 1960.

Features: Spring metal take-up spool retaining shaft. Four screw accessory shoe.

Remarks: This camera represents the third variation based on the Shanghai 58-I camera of 1958. An attempt was made to again cut production costs, by deleting the strap lugs from the camera body. The focal plane shutter was also changed slightly, in order to make repairs easier, and eliminate an adjustment problem inherent in the previous Shanghai 58 type cameras. The third version accounts for almost half of Shanghai 58-II production.

Shanghai 58-II (4th version)

The fourth and final version of the Shanghai 58-II. This one had only three screws in the accessory shoe and no dioptre adjustment.

Factory: Shanghai Camera Factory, Shanghai.

Camera Type: Split-image rangefinder with interchangeable lens, using 135 film. Bottom loading.

Taking Lens: Coated f=50mm 1:3.5, three elements in three groups. Collapsible tube with M39-1 screw thread. Focussing from 1.1m to infinity.

Viewing Lens: Single window combining split-image rangefinder and field of view for normal 50mm lens. No dioptre adjustment.

Shutter: Cloth focal plane shutter with speeds from 1 sec to 1/1000 sec, including T and B. PC type flash synch. No self timer.

Dates of Production: 1962-63?

Number Produced: 30,000?

Serial Number information: On top plate, beginning 58XXXXX.

Selling Price: 200 RMB yuan, in 1962.

Features: Spring metal take-up spool retaining shaft. Three screw accessory shoe.

Remarks: This camera represents the fourth variation based on the Shanghai 58-I camera of 1958. A final attempt was made to cut production costs by removing the dioptre adjustment and replacing the four-screw complicated accessory shoe with a much simpler three-screw model. The fourth version accounts for almost half of Shanghai 58-II production. Though production officially stopped in 1963, new cameras were to be found on the store shelves until well into the 1960s.

Shanghai (TLR)

The Shanghai twin lens reflex. It was dubbed the 58-III during pre-production.

Factory: Shanghai Camera Factory, Shanghai.

Camera Type: Twin Lens Reflex.

Taking Lens: Coated three elements in three groups f=75mm, 1:3.5, focussing from 1m to infinity.

Viewing Lens: Coated f=75mm, 1:2.8.

Shutter: Manually set between-the-lens type with speeds of 1 sec to 1/300 sec plus B. Self timer, PC type flash synch.

Dates of Production: 1960-64?

Number Produced: Tens of thousands.

Serial Number Information: Both the taking lens and the viewing lens have serial numbers around the lens bezel. The body number appears on top of the camera logo, and always begins with the digits 63XXXXX.

Selling Price: ?

Features: Folding magnifier built into the focussing hood, 12 exposures 6 x 6cm on 120 film, automatic frame counting. Focussing screen is marked in a grid pattern.

Remarks: The Shanghai TLR was originally called the 58-III while in testing stages. It is well made, and can still occasionally be found in the secondhand stores in China. In 1964, the name changed to Seagull-4, although no changes were made to the camera itself.

Shanghai 201

Factory: Shanghai Camera Factory, Shanghai.

Camera Type: Folding 120 viewfinder camera, with scale focussing.

Taking Lens: Coated 7.5cm, 1:4.5, three elements in three groups. Marked S.C. 60. Focussing from 1.2m to infinity.

Shutter: Manually set between the lens type. 1/10 sec to 1/200 sec B. No self timer, no synch.

Dates of Production: 1959?

Number Produced: ?

Serial Number Information: The camera serial number appears inside the body, stamped into the film pressure plate.

Selling Price: ?

Features: Shutter release coupled to body. Hinged masks for 6 x 6cm or 6 x 4.5cm on 120 film. Ruby window frame counting, marked for 12 and 16 frames. No double exposure prevention.

Remarks: This simple 120 folding camera is a direct copy of the Agfa Isolette of the 1950s. Because of the 201 model designation, we can assume that it was made in the Shanghai No.2 Camera Factory.

From the front and top... the Shanghai 201. Compare the script in which the camera name is written on the top plate with that on the Shanghai 202 illustrated on the next page. The style on the camera below was used for both the 201 and the first production of the 202 model.

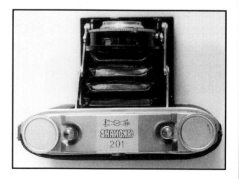

Shanghai 202

Factory: Shanghai Camera Factory, Shanghai.

Camera Type: Folding 120 viewfinder camera, with scale focussing.

Taking Lens: Coated 7.5cm, 1:4.5, three elements in three groups. Marked S.C.60. Focussing from 1.2m to infinity.

Shutter: Manually set between-the-lens type. 1/10 sec to 1/200 sec. Self timer, PC post synch.

Dates of Production: 1960-63?

Number Produced: ?

Serial Number Information: The camera serial number appears inside the body, stamped into the film pressure plate, and contains six digits.

Selling Price: ?

Features: Shutter release coupled to body. Hinged masks for 6 x 6cm or 6 x 4.5cm on 120 film. Ruby window frame counting, marked for 12 and 16 frames. No double exposure prevention.

Remarks: The 202 model is the continuation of the 201 model of 1959, with the addition of self timer and flash synch. A variation in print style used to emboss the Shanghai name on the metal top plate appears towards the end of production.

Front and top... the Shanghai 202. Note the difference in script on the top plate between this camera and the 201 model illustrated on the previous page.

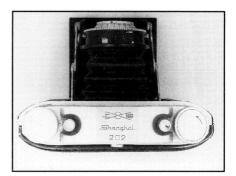

Shanghai 203

Factory: Shanghai No.2 Camera Factory, Shanghai.

Camera Type: Folding 120 camera with coupled split-image rangefinder.

Taking Lens: Coated f=75mm, 1:3.5, three elements in two groups, focussing from 1.2m to infinity.

Viewing Lens: Split-image rangefinder with field of view for 75mm lens.

Shutter: Manually set between-the-lens type 1 sec to 1/300 sec plus B. EV coupled with aperture control. Self timer and PC post synch.

Dates of Production: 1963.

Number Produced: ?

Serial Number Information: Both the lens and the camera body have a serial number. No reference to the date of production, or indication of the number produced can be inferred from these.

Selling Price: ?

Features: Coupled rangefinder, front element focussing, coupled EV scale. Film speed reminder dial, along with camera setting suggestions on top plate. Lever advance with double exposure prevention, ruby window frame counting. Built-in hinged masks for 6 x 4.5cm.

Front and top... the Shanghai 203, a short-lived precursor to the Seagull 203.

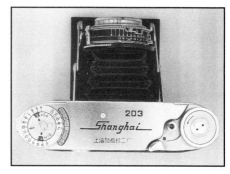

Remarks: The Shanghai 203 was the short lived precursor to the Seagull 203. Its single year of production certainly saw few cameras made. The change of marketing strategy by the Ministry of Light Industry saw the name Shanghai disappear, replaced by Seagull.

Seagull 203 (first version)

From the front and top... the first version of the Seagull 203, one of the most common 120 rollfilm cameras.

Factory: Shanghai Camera Factory, Shanghai.

Camera Type: Folding 120 camera with coupled split-image rangefinder.

Taking Lens: Coated f=75mm, 1:3.5, three elements in two groups, focussing from 1.2m to infinity.

Viewing Lens: Split-image rangefinder with field of view for 75mm lens.

Shutter: Manually set between-the-lens type with speeds of 1 sec to 1/300 sec plus B. EV coupled with aperture control. Self timer and PC post synch.

Dates of Production: 1964-75?

Number Produced: ?

Serial Number Information: Both the lens and the camera body have a serial number. No reference to the date of production, or indication of the number produced can be inferred from these.

Selling Price: 100 RMB yuan.

Features: Coupled rangefinder, front element focussing, coupled EV scale. Film speed reminder dial, along with camera setting suggestions on top plate. Lever advance with double exposure

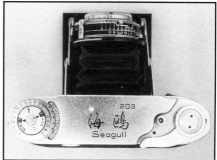

prevention, ruby window frame counting. Built in hinged masks for 6 x 4.5cm.

Remarks: The Seagull 203 (first version) was in production for about ten years with no change. It is one of the most common 120 roll film cameras found in second hand stores in China.

Seagull 203 (second version)

Factory: Shanghai Camera Factory, Shanghai.

Camera Type: Folding 120 camera with coupled split-image rangefinder.

Taking Lens: Coated f=75mm, 1:3.5, three elements in two groups, focussing from 1.2m to infinity.

Viewing Lens: Split image rangefinder with field of view for 75mm lens.

Shutter: Manually set between the lens type 1 sec to 1/300 sec plus B. Self timer and PC post synch.

Dates of Production:1976-85.

Number Produced: ?

Serial Number Information: Both the lens and the camera body have serial numbers. No reference to the date of production, or indication of the number produced can be inferred from these.

Selling Price:100 RMB yuan.

Features: Coupled rangefinder, front element focussing, plate. Lever advance with double exposure prevention, ruby window frame counting. Built in hinged masks for 6 x 4.5cm.

Remarks: The Seagull 203 (second version) was in production for about ten years. It is a very common 120 rollfilm camera to be found in second hand stores in China. It differs from the first version in several respects. It has lost the EV scale coupling. A plastic wind lever also replaces the first version's metal one. An accessory shoe holds the place previously occupied by the film reminder dial.

Seagull 203-H

From the front and top... the Seagull 203-H, last of the model 203 cameras.

Factory: Shanghai Camera Factory, Shanghai.

Camera Type: Folding 120 camera with coupled split-image rangefinder.

Taking Lens: Coated f=75mm, 1:3.5, three elements in two groups, focussing from 1.2m to infinity.

Viewing Lens: Split-image rangefinder with field of view for 75mm lens.

Shutter: Manually set between-the-lens type 1 sec to 1/300 sec plus B. Self timer.

Dates of Production: 1985-86?

Number Produced: ?

Serial Number Information: Both the lens and the camera body have serial numbers. No reference to the date of production, or indication of the number produced can be inferred from these.

Selling Price: 100 RMB yuan (but available in some stores as a closeout for 60 RMB yuan).

Features: Coupled rangefinder, front element focussing, plate. Lever advance with double exposure prevention, ruby window frame counting. Built in hinged masks for 6 x 4.5cm.

Remarks: The Seagull 203-H is the last of the 120 folding rangefinder cameras from the Shanghai Camera Factory. The H stands for the Chinese word meaning Black. The camera has a black plastic top plate, with an accessory shoe, and PC flash connection. The chrome plating used on this camera is far below the quality used on the first Seagull 203.

Seagull 9

The Seagull 9. Unlike the vast majority of 35mm cameras, it used an unusual 24 x 31mm format that allowed 42 exposures on a standard 36-exposure length film.

Factory: Shanghai No.3 Camera Factory, Shanghai.

Camera Type: Simple viewfinder camera for 35mm film.

Taking Lens: Coated f=40mm, 1:3.5, three elements, scale focussing from 0.9m to infinity.

Viewing Lens: Optical eye-level viewfinder.

Shutter: Between-the-lens type with speeds of 1 sec to 1/250 sec plus B. No self timer, no flash synch.

Dates of Production: 1974.

Number Produced: ?

Serial Number Information: The camera serial number appears on the back of the top plate, and begins 9-74XXXX. The first two digits indicate the year of production.

Selling Price: 48 RMB yuan, in 1974.

Features: Lever advance, top mounted rewind knob.

Remarks: The short-lived Seagull 9 used the unusual 24mm x 31mm negative format. This allowed 42 pictures on a roll normally having 36. This camera never caught on, and probably fewer than 5,000 were made. Most of them were sold in the Shanghai area. It is interesting to note that the Shanghai No.3 factory now makes lenses for enlargers, photocopiers, and large format cameras.

Seagull 501

From the top... the Seagull 501. Note the 35mm frame counter on the advance wheel. 'Serve The People' is visible just above.

Factory: Shanghai No.5 Camera Factory, Shanghai.

Camera Type: Simple viewfinder camera.

Taking Lens: Coated f=75mm. 1:4.5, scale focussing 1.2m to infinity.

Viewing Lens: Optical viewfinder located centrally over the taking lens. Frame lines for 6 x 6cm, 6 x 4.5cm, and 24 x 36mm visible in the finder.

Shutter: Manually set between-the-lens type, 1/10 to 1/200 sec, plus B, no self timer, no synch.

Dates of Production: 1968-69.

Number Produced: 5,000?

Serial Number Information: The serial number is located on the lens bezel, beginning with 50XXXX. The 5 may stand for the No.5 factory.

Selling price: ?

Features: The Seagull 501 camera is able to use both 120 and 135 film. The 120 film gives either 6 x 6cm or 6 x 4.5cm negatives, by use of ruby windows, and a removable metal mask. 135 film could be used by means of a special holder insert. Frames are counted by numbered increments around the large film advance knob. No provision for rewinding was made, as the film advanced from cassette to cassette.

Remarks: This camera appears to be quite rare, and the factory itself doesn't seem to have endured for a very long time. The Seagull 501 camera has been found with slogans from the Cultural Revolution on both the top plate, and the focussing scale bezel. The popular saying *Serve the People,* in Mao's own handwriting is engraved on the right hand side of the top. *Long Live Chairman Mao,* along with a slogan in Lin Biao's hand sometimes appear around the lens.

Seagull-4

Factory: Shanghai Camera Factory, Shanghai.

Camera Type: Twin Lens Reflex.

Taking Lens: Coated three elements in three groups f=75mm, 1:3.5, focussing from 1m to infinity.

Viewing Lens: Coated f=75mm, 1:2.8.

Shutter: Manually set between-the-lens type with speeds of 1 sec to 1/300 sec plus B. Self timer, PC type flash synch. Marked *China, Shanghai* in English and Chinese.

Dates of Production: 1964-?

Number Produced: Tens of thousands.

Serial Number Information: Both the taking lens and the viewing lens have serial numbers around the lens bezel. The body number appears on top of the camera logo, and always begins with 4-63XXXXXX.

Selling Price: ?

Features: Folding magnifier built into the focussing hood, 12 exposures 6 x 6cm on 120 film, automatic frame counting. The focussing screen is marked in a grid pattern.

The Seagull-4 twin lens reflex. Compare this model with the Shanghai TLR.

Remarks: The Seagull-4 TLR is the same camera as the Shanghai TLR of 1963 and earlier. The Seagull name was adopted for use in the export market.

Seagull-4A

Factory: Shanghai Camera Factory, Shanghai.

Camera Type: Twin Lens Reflex.

Taking Lens: Coated three elements in three groups f=75mm, 1:3.5, focussing from 1m to infinity.

Viewing Lens: Coated f=75mm, 1:2.8.

Shutter: Between-the-lens type automatically set upon film advance, with speeds of 1 sec to 1/300 sec plus B. Self timer, PC type flash synch. Marked *China, Shanghai* in English and Chinese.

Dates of Production: ?

Number Produced: Tens of thousands.

Viewing Lens: The viewing lens has a serial number around the lens bezel. The body number appears on top of the camera logo, and always begins with 4A-XXXXXXXX.

Selling Price: Originally 165 RMB yuan, with hard leather case, but discounted to 65 RMB yuan in 1988.

Features: Folding magnifier built into the focussing hood, 12 exposures 6 x 6cm on 120 film, automatic frame counting. Crank type film advance. The focussing screen is marked in a grid pattern.

The Seagull-4A twin lens reflex. It offered several improvements on the Seagull-4.

Remarks: The Seagull-4A TLR offers some improvements on the Seagull 4 TLR. Cameras with a red dot after the body number did not pass quality control, and were to be offered for sale on the domestic market only.

Seagull-4B

Factory: Shanghai Camera Factory, Shanghai.

Camera Type: Twin Lens Reflex.

Taking Lens: Coated three elements in three groups f=75mm, 1:3.5, focussing from 1m to infinity.

Viewing Lens: Coated f=75mm, 1:3.5.

Shutter: Manually set between-the-lens type with speeds of 1 sec to 1/300 sec plus B. Self timer, PC type flash synch. Marked *China, Shanghai* in English and Chinese.

Dates of Production?

Number Produced: Tens of thousands.

Serial Number Information: The taking lens has a serial number around the lens bezel. The body number appears on top of the camera logo, and always begins with 4B-XXXXXXX.

Selling Price: 120 RMB yuan with leather case.

The Seagull-4B twin lens reflex. It became one of the most prolific TLRs in China.

Features: Folding magnifier built into the focussing hood, 12 exposures 6 x 6cm, or 16 exposures 6 x 4.5cm on 120 film, through the use of a removable metal mask, and double ruby windows. The focussing screen is marked with the field of view for 6 x 6cm, and 6 x 4.5cm.

Remarks: The Seagull-4B TLR is the inexpensive version of the Seagull 4A, using ruby windows instead of automatic advance. Many other Chinese TLRs are based on this same body design. This is one of the most common TLRs found on the used market in China today.

Seagull-4B-1

Factory: Shanghai Camera Factory, Shanghai.

Camera Type: Twin Lens Reflex.

Taking Lens: Coated three elements in three groups f=75mm, 1:3.5, focussing from 1m to infinity.

Viewing Lens: Coated f=75mm, 1:3.5.

Shutter: Manually set between-the-lens type with speeds of 1 sec to 1/300 sec plus B. Self timer, PC type flash synch. Marked *China, Shanghai* in English and Chinese.

Dates of Production: ?

Number Produced: ?

Serial Number Information: The body number appears on top of the camera logo, and always begins with 4BI-XXXXXXX. The taking lens has its own serial number around the lens bezel.

Selling Price:165 RMB yuan, with hard leather case, recently discounted to 65 RMB yuan.

Features: Folding magnifier built into the focussing hood, 12 exposures 6 x 6cm, or 16 exposures 6 x 4.5cm on 120 film, through the use of a removable metal mask, and double ruby windows. Fresnel focussing screen with central ground spot, marked with field of view for 6 x 6cm, and 6 x 4.5cm negatives. Acces-

The Seagull-4B-1 twin lens reflex, one of the last Seagull TLRs on the market.

sory shoe mounted on the left side of the camera body.

Remarks: The Seagull-4B-1 is one of the last Seagull TLR cameras on the market. Its Fresnel screen (the only difference between it and the Seagull-4B) makes focussing much easier. This camera is no longer being produced and dealers are trying to remove unsold cameras to make room for new stock.

Seagull-4C

Factory: Shanghai Camera Factory, Shanghai.

Camera Type: Twin Lens Reflex.

Taking Lens: Coated three elements in three groups f=75mm, 1:3.5, focussing from 1m to infinity.

Viewing Lens: Coated f=75mm, 1:3.5.

Shutter: Manually set between-the-lens type with speeds of 1 sec to 1/300 sec plus B. Self timer, PC type flash synch.

Dates of Production: ?

Number Produced: ?

Serial Number Information: Both the taking lens and the viewing lens have serial numbers around the lens bezel. The body number appears on top of the camera logo, and always begins with 4C-XXXXXXX.

Selling Price: ?

Features: Folding magnifier built into the focussing hood, 12 exposures 6 x 6cm on 120 film, 35mm film usable with special adaptor, built in frame counter for 35mm. Focussing screen marked for 6 x 6cm, 6 x 4.5cm, and vertical full-frame 35mm negatives.

The Seagull-4C twin lens reflex. Note the 35mm frame counter and release catch under the advance knob.

Remarks: The Seagull-4C camera is a Seagull-4B TLR modified for use with 35mm film, in addition to 120 rollfilm. A Yashica 635 is said to have been the inspiration for its design. It was not very popular, but did offer the photo taking public a way to use 35mm colour film. (Kits are still being sold to allow the use of 35mm film in Seagull-4B cameras).

Hong Qi 20 (Red Flag 20)

Factory: Shanghai No.2 Camera Factory, Shanghai.

Camera Type: Split-image rangefinder with interchangeable lenses.

Taking Lens: Normally supplied with a coated f=50mm, 1:1.4 copy of the Leitz Summilux lens. An f=35mm, 1:1.4 (also a Summilux copy) wide angle lens and an f=90, 1:2.0 (a copy of Summicron) telephoto lens were also available.

Viewing Lens: Split-image rangefinder with bright line indication of field of view for each of the three lenses available. The correct frame line is selected automatically when a lens is mounted, or can be operated selected by use of an external lever.

Shutter: Cloth focal plane type, with speeds of 1 sec to 1/1000 sec. plus B. Self timer and M and X synch.

Dates of Production:1971-77.

Number Produced: Less than 200 (and even fewer of the wide angle and telephoto lenses were made).

Serial Number Information: Located on the back of the top plate, on the camera body, and around the lens bezel for the

The Hong Qi 20 with all three lenses. The 90mm lens is mounted.

lenses, the first two digits indicate the year of manufacture.

Selling Price: More than 6000 RMB yuan with leather ever ready case, lens hood and lens cap.

Features: Film speed reminder around the rewind knob in DIN only. Leica bayonet mount.

Remarks: The Red Flag 20 camera was a direct copy of the Leica M4. It was ordered into production by Chiang Ching, the wife of Mao, and the leader of the Gang of Four.

DFAB

Factory: Shanghai Camera Factory, Shanghai.

Camera Type: 35mm special purpose camera.

Taking Lens: For CRT photography, coated f=58mm 1:2 with focus adjustable from about 2m to 0.5m, using a scale from 0-9, but available without lens for use as a microscope camera.

Viewing Lens: No provision for a viewing system was made on this camera.

Shutter: Cloth focal plane shutter with speeds of 1 sec to 1/60 sec plus B. No self timer, no flash synch.

Dates of Production: 1970-77?

Number Produced: Several hundred?

Serial Number Information: The serial number is located on the back of the top plate, and another serial number appears around the lens bezel.

Selling Price: ?

Remarks: This special purpose camera was made for use in the laboratory, where focussing was not needed, and where exposures of faster than 1/60 sec were not used. This camera is like the DFC camera, except for the choice of shutter speeds available.

The DFAB, a special-purpose camera made for CRT photography in the laboratory where no focussing control was needed.

DFC

Factory: Shanghai Camera Factory, Shanghai.

Camera Type: 35mm special purpose camera.

Taking Lens: For CRT photography, coated f=58mm 1:2 as DFAB, but available without lens for use as a microscope camera.

Viewing lens: No provision for a viewing system was made on this camera.

Shutter: Cloth focal plane shutter with only B setting. No self timer, no flash synch.

Dates of Production:1970-77?

Number Produced: Several hundred?

Serial Number Information: The serial number is located on the back of the top plate, and another serial number appears around the lens bezel.

Selling Price: ?

Remarks: This special purpose camera was made for use in the laboratory, where foucssing was not needed, and where long exposures were expected. Otherwise this camera is like the DFAB camera made at the same time.

Dong Feng (East Wind)

Factory: Shanghai No.2 Camera Factory, Shanghai.

Camera Type:120 rollfilm Single Lens Reflex.

Taking Lens: Coated f=80mm. 1:2.8 normal lens, f=150mm, 1:4.0 telephoto lens, and f=50mm, 1:4.0 wide angle lens.

Viewing Lens: Removable waist-level finder with Fresnel lens.

Shutter: Between-the-lens type, 1 sec to 1/1000(!) sec plus B on the normal lens, 1 sec to 1/500 plus B on the accessory lenses. (An extra spring had to be separately tensioned when using the 1/1000 sec. Instructions caution not to tension this spring when using the slower speeds.)

Dates of Production:1970

Number Produced: Fewer than 50?

Serial Number Information: There is no serial number on the camera body. The lens number is located on the bezel, the first two digits indicating the number of years since liberation the lens was made.

Selling Price:18,000 RMB yuan with three lenses, special filters, and carrying

The Dong Feng with all three lenses, certainly a copy of the Hasselblad 500 series.

case. (Though never on store shelves, cameras were sold direct from the factory.)

Features: Removable 120 rollfilm back for 12 exposures 6 x 6cm.

Remarks: Certainly a copy of the Hasselblad 500 series camera, the Dong Feng went the extra step with a 1/1000 sec shutter. Few were made, and those that remain in service show their years of wear. Most suffer from broken linking tabs, which shear off if the lens and body are not cocked when attaching the lens, exactly like Hasselblad.

Seagull DF-1 (Model 102)

Factory: Shanghai General Camera Factory, Shanghai.

Camera Type: 35mm Single lens reflex, with interchangeable lenses.

Taking Lens: Coated f=58mm, 1:2, focussing from 0.6m to infinity.

Viewing Lens: Non-removable pentaprism for through-the-lens viewing, central split-image rangefinder surrounded by a microprism collar on a fixed ground glass.

Shutter: Cloth focal plane type with speeds of 1 sec to 1/1000 sec, plus B. X flash synch between 1/30 sec and 1/60 sec.

Dates of Production: 1969 present.

Number Produced: Tens of thousands.

Serial Number Information: The camera body number is located on the top plate, and begins with the model number, in this case 102-XXXXX. The lens number is on the lens bezel.

Selling Price: 580 RMB yuan.

The Seagull DF-1 Model 102. Like other Seagull models, this one was based on a Minolta design.

Features: Hot shoe, Minolta type bayonet mount, not equipped with a light meter.

Remarks: The Seagull DF-1 was made in three models, the 102, 104, and ETM. All three cameras were based on Minolta designs. One of the most prolific SLR cameras in China. A 135mm telephoto lens and a 35mm wide angle lens to fit Minolta mount were made at a factory in Changchun. The 90mm lens from the Great Wall DF-2 could also be found, in a special focussing mount.

Model ZA

Factory: Shanghai No.3 Camera Factory, Shanghai.

Camera Type: Special purpose microscope camera for 60mm size negatives, can be used with a Seagull DFAB, or DFC special purpose cameras or with the Seagull DF-1 35mm SLR.

Taking Lens: Uses the objectives of a microscope along with 4x and 6.4x eyepieces and a single element magnifier.

Viewing Lens: Through-the-lens viewing and focussing by use of a sliding mirror. The mirror is manually removed from the light path when the exposure is made.

Shutter: Metal, manually set leaf-type shutter, B setting only, fired by a cable release.

Dates of Production: 1975-80?

Number produced: Several hundred.

Serial Number Information: The camera serial number is engraved on a metal plate on the body of the camera. The first two digits indicate the year of production.

Selling Price: 685 RMB yuan, including wooden case, 4x and 6.4x eyepieces, and three film holders.

Features: Interchangeable film holder using Minolta MD type mount. Diopter adjustment on the viewing eyepiece.

Remarks: 120 rollfilm was cut to fit into the film holders of this camera. A round image 60mm in diameter was obtained. Not a very popular camera the Model ZA had very limited sales. As late as 1988, new cameras were gathering dust on some store shelves.

Seagull CL-A

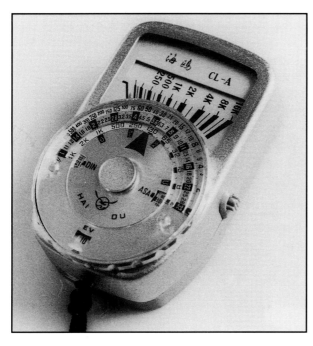

The Seagull CL-A light meter, the only meter made in recent times in China. It is a copy of a Weston meter of the 1950s.

Factory: Shanghai No.2 Photographic Equipment Factory, Shanghai.

Dates of Production: ?

Number Produced: ?

Serial Number Information: Four digits, engraved on the back plate.

Selling Price: 160 RMB yuan.

Type: Hand-held, metal-bodied meter for incident or reflected light metering. High and low scale switch, and reading lock, with EV scale from 2 to 21. Conversion scale on the back from DIN to Weston (ASA). It was sold with a fitted vinyl case, battery cover removal tool, and carrying cord.

Remarks: This light meter is the only light meter made in recent days in China. (A meter was made for the Shanghai 58-II camera, for use on its accessory shoe, but it was not long in production, and not many were sold). It can still be found on camera store shelves in Shanghai. It appears well made, and is a copy of a Weston meter of the 1950s. It is marked in both DIN (9-33) and ASA (6-1600).

Cameras from Nanjing

THE CHANG CHIANG

Zi Jin Shan (Purple Mountain)

Front and back... the Zi Jin Shan. Note the arm beside the lens, used to lower the mirror.

Factory: Nanjing Motion Picture Equipment Factory, Nanjing.

Camera Type: 35mm SLR with interchangeable lens.

Taking Lens: Coated f=50mm, 1:3.5, focussing from 1m to infinity. M39-1 screw mount, lens to film plane distance the same as for Zenit SLR cameras. Approx. thirty 1:2.8 lenses were made at the end of production.

Viewing Lens: Pentaprism without instant return mirror.

Shutter: Cloth focal plane type with speeds of 1/25 sec to 1/500 sec plus B. No flash synch, no self timer.

Dates of Production: 1959-60.

Number Produced: Less than 1,000.

Serial Number Information: The serial number appears on the lens bezel, the first two digits indicate the year of production.

Selling Price: 200 RMB yuan.

Features: Strap lugs on the body, removable back for film loading.

Remarks: This was the first Chinese 35mm SLR to be marketed, and it has a very interesting history. The mirror return is not connected to the film advance, and the mirror must be lowered after each exposure by means of the lever located next to the lens.

Zi Jin Shan
(Purple Mountain)

Factory: Nanjing Motion Picture Equipment Factory, Nanjing.

Camera Type: Twin Lens Reflex.

Taking Lens: No information available.

Shutter: No information available.

Dates of Production: 1959.

Number Produced: ?

Serial Number Information: ?

Selling Price: ?

Features: No information is available.

Remarks: This camera suffered the same fate as the Zi Jin Shan 35mm SLR. Though of high quality, production was stopped before it could really be sold in any great numbers.

Chang Chiang (Yangtze River)

The Chang Chiang, one method of spelling Yangtze River *before the standardisation of Romanized spelling was established by the Chinese government.*

Factory: Guang Optical Instrument Factory, Nanjing.

Camera Type: 35mm Rangefinder with interchangeable lens.

Taking Lens: Coated f=50mm, 1:2.8, focussing from 1m to infinity.

Viewing Lens: Split image rangefinder with field of view for 50mm lens, dioptre adjustment.

Shutter: Cloth focal plane type with speeds of 1/25 sec to 1/500 sec plus B. No self timer, PC flash synch.

Dates of Production: 1958.

Number Produced: Less than 100.

Serial Number Information: The body number is located on the back of the top plate, and begins 1958XX, 1958 being the year of manufacture.

Selling Price: This camera was never sold on the open market.

Features: Accessory shoe, and M39 screw lens mount.

Remarks: The Chang Chiang camera was made as a test, to study the possibility of producing a quality 35mm rangefinder camera to compete with the Shanghai 58-I. It is a direct copy of the Russian FED-2, type two. In 1959 it reached the marketplace without much change, and was sold until production ceased in 1961. The Romanized name *Chang Chiang* appears on the top plate, and *Made In China* is in English on the front of the top plate.

Nanjing

The Nanjing camera (left), compared with the Russian Fed-2 (right). Note that this Fed-2 is the first version. The second version had flash synch and a rigid lens exactly as the Nanjing and the Chang Chiang.

Factory: Guang Optical Instrument Factory, Nanjing.

Camera Type: 35mm Rangefinder with interchangeable lens, M39-1 screw mount.

Taking Lens: Coated f=50mm, 1:2.8, focussing from 1m to infinity.

Viewing Lens: Split image rangefinder with field of view for 50mm lens, dioptre adjustment.

Shutter: Cloth focal plane type with speeds of 1/25 sec to 1/500 sec plus B. No self timer, PC flash synch.

Dates of Production: 1959-61?

Number Produced: Less than 2,000?

Serial Number Information: The body number is located on the top plate, and is preceded by M1-.

Selling Price: 200 RMB yuan, with leather eveready case.

Features: Accessory shoe, and M39 screw lens mount.

Remarks: The Nanjing Camera reached market in 1959, and came about as the result of the manufacturing test carried out with the Chang Chiang of 1958. The only real difference between the two cameras being the use of a stamped metal top plate on the Nanjing instead of the cast aluminium housing of the Chang Chiang. The Nanjing camera was also known as the Nanjing 58-II, a take-off of the Shanghai 58-II. Most of the cameras sold stayed in the Nanjing area.

Cameras from Tianjin

THE CHENGUANG

Wooden View Camera

Front and back... the Wooden View Camera. The back view shows the wooden rollfilm holder for 120 film in position.

Factory: Yung Mao (Prosperous) Photographic Material and Equipment Factory, in the alley next to the Da Zhong Theatre, South City, Tianjin.

Camera Type: Wooden view camera, with revolving back and rising front.

Taking Lens: ?

Viewing Lens: Removable ground glass back marked for 3 x 4.5 inches, and 2.25 x 3.25 inches.

Shutter: ?

Dates of Production: 1955?

Number Produced: One at a time, hand-made in workshops by craftsmen, total quantity unknown.

Serial Number Information: No serial number appears on this camera.

Selling Price: ?

Features: Rising and tilting front, revolving back, accessory wooden 120 rollfilm holder.

Remarks: Typical of the wooden view cameras made in workshops where one man was responsible for construction of the camera from start to finish. Imported mahogany from the Philippines, and hand-made chrome plated brass fixtures were used in its construction. Such care was taken in its manufacture that all the screw head slots are aligned. It is a much better made Wooden View Camera than those which were produced after the Cultural Revolution.

July First*

The July First camera, front and back. Note the knurled focussing wheel on the back.

Factory: Tianjin Camera Factory, Tianjin.

Camera Type: Folding 120 camera with coupled split-image rangefinder.

Taking Lens: Coated f=7.5cm, 1:3.5 (stopping down to f/32). Three elements in three groups, non focussing.

Viewing Lens: Combined viewfinder/ rangefinder showing field of view for 74mm lens.

Shutter: Five blade between-the-lens type with speeds of 1 sec to 1/300 sec plus B. Self timer and PC synch.

Dates of Production: Late 1956.

Number Produced: About 40.

Serial Number Information: The camera serial number is located on the top plate, numbered 000XX.

Selling Price: 200 RMB yuan, with case. (This was the projected selling price, but the camera never came on the open market.)

Features: Accessory shoe on top plate. Coupled automatic frame counter for 12 exposures on 120 film.

Remarks: This aluminium-bodied camera bears a strong likeness to the Mamiya Six from which it was copied. It even uses the same unusual film plane focussing as the Mamiya Six. Since it has a frame counter coupled to the advance, and used a single red window for positioning the first frame, no provision was made for 6 x 4.5cm size exposures. The July 1st camera never made it to the market place. It was just too expensive to make. This is 'officially' the first camera made after 'liberation', though the Da Lai 35mm was announced a couple of months before.

***Date of the founding of the Chinese Communist Party, in 1921.**

Xing Fu (Happiness)

Factory: Tianjin Camera Product Factory, Tianjin.

Camera Type: Simple box camera.

Taking Lens: Uncoated two element, fixed focus from 1.6m to infinity. Choice of two stops, f/11, and f/22.

Viewing Lens: Eye-level direct-vision finder.

Shutter: Between-the-lens with speeds of 1/25 sec and B.

Dates of Production: 1959.

Number Produced: ?

Serial Number Information: This camera carried no serial number.

Selling Price: ?

Features: 12 exposures on 120 film.

Remarks: This camera was announced as being good for a beginner. It is the only known example of a true box camera produced in China. It was dropped from production when people didn't respond to the idea of a simple, cheap camera. Plans for an improved Xing Fu-2 were dropped, even though the camera itself was announced, and a few test cameras were sold.

Front and back... the Xing Fu, the only known example of a true Chinese box camera.

Xing Fu-2 (Happiness-2)

This broken example of a Xing Fu-2 was salvaged from the rubbish bin for 1 RMB yuan. Though obviously incomplete and broken, no other example has been found.

Factory: Tianjin Camera Product Factory, Tianjin.

Camera Type: Simple viewfinder camera.

Taking Lens: Symmetrical lens un-coated, fixed focus from 2m to infinity, f/11, f/16 and f/22.

Viewing Lens: Direct-vision eye-level finder.

Shutter: Between-the-lens type with speeds of 1/50 sec and B. No self timer. No flash synch.

Dates of Production: 1960?

Number Produced: Few?

Serial Number Information: No serial number appeared on this camera.

Selling Price: Announced price of 40 RMB yuan.

Features: 12 exposures 6 x 6cm or 16 exposures 6 x 4.5cm on 120 film.

Remarks: The second version of the Xing Fu camera was meant to be an improvement on the original, based on customer opinions about the first camera. The basic box camera design was changed to a more beautiful 35mm type body style. Unfortunately, it never made it on the market.

Eastar

The Eastar twin lens reflex. Note the similarity with the Seagull 4B.

Factory: Tianjin Camera Factory, Tianjin.

Camera Type: Twin Lens Reflex.

Taking Lens: Coated f=75mm, 1:3.5, focussing from 1m to infinity.

Viewing Lens: Coated f=75mm, 1:3.5.

Shutter: Manually set between-the-lens type with speeds of 1 sec to 1/300 sec plus B. Self timer and PC flash synch.

Dates of Production: 1977.

Number Produced: ?

Serial Number Information: The body number is located above the camera name, and begins with F-. Both the taking lens and viewing lens have their own numbers around the lens bezel.

Selling Price: 165 RMB yuan, with hard leather case, recently discounted to 70 RMB yuan.

Features: 12 exposures 6 x 6cm or 16 exposures 6 x 4.5cm on 120 rollfilm, through the use of a metal mask insert and red windows.

Remarks: The Eastar TLR is quite commonly found in secondhand stores in the Beijing area. The only camera found more often is the Seagull-4B upon which the Eastar is based. The name Eastar is really a poor translation of the camera's Chinese name, *Dong Feng*. The meaning is closer to Eastern, (literally, the region in the East).

Eastar

The Eastar 135, originally copied from Yashica and now one of the longest-running products in the Chinese photo industry.

Factory: Tianjin Camera Factory, Tianjin.

Camera Type: 35mm rangefinder with fixed lens.

Taking Lens: Coated f=50mm, 1:2.8, focussing from 0.8m to infinity.

Viewing Lens: Combined rangefinder/viewfinder showing field of view for 50mm lens, parallax-corrected bright line frame.

Shutter: Between-the-lens type with speeds of 1 sec to 1/300 sec and B. Self timer and PC type flash synch.

Dates of Production: 1965-present.

Number Produced: Tens of thousands.

Serial Number Information: The body number is located on the top plate, the lens number is on the lens bezel.

Selling Price: 265 RMB yuan, with case.

Features: Film speed reminder in ASA and DIN.

Remarks: One of the longest running products in the Chinese photo industry. Originally copied from the Yashica Minister D, the Eastar is commonly found on second-hand store shelves in all the cities of China. The current model is all black, giving it the pro look.

Chenguang (Dawn)

Factory: Tianjin Camera Factory, Tianjin.

Camera Type: Single Lens Reflex with interchangeable lens.

Taking Lens: Coated f=50mm, 1:3.5, focussing from 1m to infinity. 45mm screw mount, preset diaphragm.

Viewing Lens: Pentaprism with non-interchangeable ground glass screen.

Shutter: Cloth focal plane type, with speeds of 1/30 sec to 1/500 sec plus B. Self timer and PC flash synch at 1/30 sec.

Dates of Production: 1959-64.

Number Produced: About 170.

Serial Number Information: The body number is located on the back of the top plate, the first two digits indicate the year of production. The lens has its own number around the bezel, also with the first two numbers being the year of production.

Selling Price: This camera was never officially sold, though some members of the factory had the chance to buy them. At least one found its way to the Public Security Office in Wuhan, Hubei Province.

Features: Non-instant return mirror, opening back for film loading, and film speed reminder around the rewind knob, in ASA and DIN.

The Chenguang. Note the shutter release on the front of the body above the self timer.

Remarks: Not a copy of any particular camera, the Chenguang was Tianjin's attempt at a first class SLR. It was originally designed at Zhejiang University, after a conference held there in 1958. It was part of the Great Leap Forward, and along with the rest of the programs of that period, it failed. The model number was said to have changed every year - i.e. 1962 = 621, 1959 = 591, but serial number information does not bear this out. One photograph exists showing a Chenguang with a light metering cell on the front. It is said that this cell was just for show, and never was actually installed.

Cameras from other factories

THE HONG QI CINE CAMERA

Emei*

Factory: People's Liberation Army Factory, Sichuan Province.

Camera Type: Twin Lens Reflex.

Taking Lens: Coated three elements in three groups f=75mm, 1:3.5, focussing from 1m to infinity.

Viewing Lens: Coated f=75mm, 1:3.5.

Shutter: Manually set between-the-lens type with speeds of 1 sec to 1/300 sec plus B. Self timer, PC type flash synch. Marked *Sichuan, China* in English and Chinese characters.

Dates of Production: 1968.

Number Produced: Less than 2,000?

Serial Number Information: The body number appears on top of the camera logo, and always begins with SF-1-19XXXXXX. (The first two digits in the main body of the serial number, 19, indicate the number of years after liberation that the camera was produced - i.e. 1949 + 19 = 1968). The taking lens and the viewing lens each have their own serial number around the lens bezel, beginning with 19XXXXXX.

Selling Price: ?

Features: Folding magnifier built into the focussing hood, 12 exposures 6 x 6cm,

The Emei twin lens reflex. The few made were sold in the West of China.

or 16 exposures 6 x 4.5cm on 120 film, through the use of a removable metal mask, and double ruby windows. Focussing screen marked with field of view for 6 x 6cm and 6 x 4.5cm negatives.

Remarks: The Emei TLR is the only known model produced during the Cultural Revolution by a People's Liberation Army factory. Not many were produced, and those which were made were sold in the West of China.

***Named after the famous Emei mountain.**

Hua Ying
(Sparkling & Transparent)

Factory: Huaguang Instrument Factory, Chongqing, Sichuan Province.

Camera Type: Twin Lens Reflex.

Taking Lens: Coated f=75mm, 1:3.5, three elements in three groups.

Viewing Lens: Coated f=75mm, 1:3.5.

Shutter: Manually set between-the-lens type with speeds of 1 sec to 1/300 plus B, self timer and PC synch.

Dates of Production: ?

Number Produced: ?

Serial Number Information: Located on the top of the name plate, beginning with Y-. The taking lens and the viewing lens also have their own numbers around the lens bezel.

Selling Price: 129 RMB yuan, but recently discounted to 65 RMB yuan, with hard leather case.

Features: 12 exposures 6 x 6cm or 16 exposures 6 x 4.5cm on 120 rollfilm, by use of a metal insert, and red windows. Ground glass is lined showing field for 6 x 4.5cm negative.

The Hua Ying twin lens reflex... the same body and style as the Seagull-4B.

Remarks: The Hua Ying TLR uses the same body style as the Seagull-4B. Although it is made in Western China, it was sold as far away as Beijing.

Hua Zhong (Central China)

Factory: Hua Zhong Precision Instrument Factory, Hubei province.

Camera Type: Twin Lens Reflex.

Taking Lens: Coated f=75mm, 1:3.5, three elements in three groups.

Viewing Lens: Coated f=75mm, 1:3.5.

Shutter: Manually set between-the-lens type with speeds of 1 sec to 1/300 plus B, self timer and PC synch.

Dates of Production: ?

Number Produced: ?

Serial Number Information: Located on top of the name plate.

Selling Price: 135 RMB yuan, but recently discounted to 65 RMB yuan with hard leather case. This camera is no longer in production.

Features: 12 exposures 6 x 6cm or 16 exposures 6 x 4.5cm on 120 rollfilm, by use of a metal insert, and red windows. Ground glass is lined showing field for 6 x 4.5cm negative. Accessory shoe mounted on the right side.

The Hua Zhong twin lens reflex... another camera that was based on he popular Seagull-4B

Remarks: The Hua Zhong is another camera based on the Seagull-4B, so popular in China. It is entirely unremarkable, and often found in second hand stores for 40 RMB yuan or less.

Mudan (Peony)

Factory: Dandong Camera Factory.

Camera Type: Twin Lens Reflex.

Taking Lens: Coated f=75mm, 1:3.5, three elements in three groups.

Viewing Lens: Coated f=75mm, 1:3.5.

Shutter: Manually set between-the-lens type with speeds of 1 sec to 1/300 plus B, self timer and PC synch.

Dates of Production: ?

Number Produced: ?

Serial Number Information: Located on the top of the name plate, the first two digits indicate the year of production.

Selling Price: 129 RMB yuan, but recently discounted to 65 RMB yuan, with hard leather case.

Features: 12 exposures 6 x 6cm or 16 exposures 6 x 4.5cm on 120 rollfilm, by use of a metal insert, and red windows. Ground glass is lined showing field for 6 x 4.5cm negative.

The Mudan twin lens reflex, often found in Chinese 'Friendship Stores' - special places for tourists to shop.

Remarks: The Mudan TLR uses the same basic body design of the Seagull-4B. This camera can often be found in the Friendship Stores, special stores where tourists shop, and are required to use foreign exchange certificates when paying for purchases.

Qingdao SF-2

Two versions of the Qingdao twin lens reflex. Note the difference in name design

Factory: Qingdao General Camera Factory, Qingdao.

Camera Type: Twin Lens Reflex.

Taking Lens: Coated f=75mm, 1:3.5, three elements in three groups, focussing from 1m to infinity, stopping down to f/32.

Viewing Lens: Coated f=75mm, 1:3.5.

Shutter: Manually set between-the-lens type with speeds of 1 sec to 1/500 plus B, self timer and PC synch.

Dates of Production: 1975-84?

Number Produced: ?

Serial Number Information: Located on the taking lens bezel. The first two digits indicate the year of production.

Selling Price: 135 RMB yuan, with hard leather case.

Features: 12 exposures 6 x 6cm or 16 exposures 6 x 4.5cm on 120 rollfilm, by use of a metal insert, and red windows. Ground glass is lined showing field for 6 x 4.5cm negative. Shutter lock around the release button.

Remarks: The Qingdao camera is made in the port city of the same name. It is modelled after Rolleiflex cameras of the 1960s, and shows shutter speeds and f-stops in a small window on top of the viewing lens. It also uses an imported Copal-XV shutter.

<u>Youyi</u> (<u>Friendship</u>)

Factory: Wuhan Camera Factory, Hankou, Hubei Province.

Camera Type: Twin Lens Reflex.

Taking Lens: Coated f=75mm, 1:3.5, three elements in three groups.

Viewing Lens: Coated f=75mm, 1:3.5.

Shutter: Manually set between-the-lens type with speeds of 1 sec to 1/300 plus B, self timer and PC synch, plus hot shoe mounted on the right side.

Dates of Production: 1975-86?

Number Produced: ?

Serial Number Information: Located on top of the name plate.

Selling Price: 129 RMB yuan, but recently discounted to 65 RMB yuan, with hard leather case.

Features: 12 exposures 6 x 6cm or 16 exposures 6 x 4.5cm on 120 rollfilm, by use of a metal insert, and red windows. Ground glass is lined showing field for 6 x 4.5cm negative.

The Youyi twin lens reflex. Note the author's birthdate as a serial number above the camera name.

Remarks: The Youyi camera appears as several incarnations. Some have the name in Pinyin romanized spelling, others use Chinese characters. One version even had *Friendship* in English. It was sold mostly in the Wuhan area. This camera is based on the Seagull-4B body style, like so many other Chinese TLRs.

Dalian

Factory: ? Camera Factory, Dalian.

Camera Type: Twin Lens Reflex.

Taking Lens: Coated three elements in three groups f=75mm, 1:3.5, focussing from 1m to infinity.

Viewing Lens: Coated f=75mm, 1:2.8.

Shutter: Manually set between-the-lens type with speeds of 1 sec to 1/300 sec plus B, self timer, PC type flash synch.

Dates of Production: 1968?

Number Produced: ?

Serial Number Information: The camera number is located above the logo. The taking lens and the viewing lens also have their own numbers around the bezel. The first two digits indicate the number of years after liberation that the camera was produced. (19 + 1949 = 1968).

Selling Price: ?

Features: Folding magnifier built into the focussing hood, 12 exposures 6 x 6cm on 120 rollfilm, 35mm film usable with special adaptor, built in frame counter for 35mm. Focussing screen marked for 6 x 6cm, 6 x 4.5cm, and vertical full frame 35mm negatives.

The Dalian twin lens reflex. Note the frame counter and release button for 35mm film beneath the film advance knob.

Remarks: The Seagull-4C provided the basic body design for the Dalian camera. The only real difference being the use of a coated f=75mm. 1:2.8 viewing lens, instead of the 1:3.5 used on the Seagull-4C. No information has been forthcoming concerning the factory which made this camera. It may have been a short lived attempt which died in 1969, when the worst of the Cultural Revolution was over.

Five Goats

Factory: Guangzhou Camera Factory, Guangdon Province.

Camera Type: Twin Lens Reflex.

Taking Lens: Coated f=75mm, 1:3.5, focussing from 1m to infinity.

Viewing Lens: Coated f=75mm, 1:3.5.

Shutter: Manually set between-the-lens type with speeds of 1/25 sec to 1/250 sec, plus B, self timer and PC flash synch. Rim set type shutter instead of the common lever set.

Dates of Production: 1970.

Number Produced: Less than 3,000.

Serial Number Information: The camera serial number is located around the taking lens, the first two digits indicate the year of production.

Selling Price: ?

Features: 12 exposures 6 x 6cm on 120 rollfilm.

The Five Goats twin lens reflex. The camera was originally to have had automatic frame counting, but the idea proved too complicated and expensive.

Remarks: The Five Goats camera is the direct predecessor of the Pearl River TLR. They differ in that Five Goats has provision for only 12 frames 6 x 6cm, while the Pearl River allows 12 or 16 frames, and the former uses the Rollei bayonette type filter mount, contrasting with the screw thread mount used on the latter. Originally, Five Goats was to have been equipped with automatic frame counting, evidenced by the starting arrows for positioning the beginning of the film roll. This proved to be too complicated and expensive, and was never put into the cameras made for sale. The name Five Goats actually is a rather poor translation, it should have been Five Rams, the symbol of Guangdon Province.

Pearl River

Factory: Guangdong Camera Factory, Guangdon Province.

Camera Type: Twin Lens Reflex.

Taking Lens: Coated f=75mm, 1:3.5, focussing from 1m to infinity.

Viewing Lens: Coated f=75mm, 1:3.5.

Shutter: Manually set between-the-lens type with speeds of 1/25 sec to 1/250 sec, plus B, self timer and PC flash synch. Rim set type shutter instead of the common lever set.

Dates of Production: ?

Number Produced: ?

Serial Number Information: Both the taking lens and the viewing lens have a serial number around the lens bezel. The first two digits indicate the year of production.

Selling Price: ?

Features: 12 exposures 6 x 6cm, or 16 exposures 6 x 4.5cm on 120 rollfilm, by use of two red windows and a metal mask insert. Film reminder built into the focussing knob.

Remarks: The Pearl River is named for the river which flows through the Guangdong delta, where it is made. It has more plastic parts than most Seagull-4B type Chinese cameras, and the shutter has no

The Pearl River twin lens reflex, named after the river which flows through the Guangdong delta, where the camera is made.

slow speeds. The Chinese have used this camera for export, and it contains some parts made in Japan. Both the name, and *Made In China* appear in English, there are no Chinese characters used. Originally the Pearl River was called the Five Goats.

Changle

The Chinese Changle (left) is a direct copy of the Russian Lubitel (right).

Factory: Xibei (Northwest) Optical Technical Factory, Xian.

Camera Type: Twin Lens Reflex.

Taking Lens: Coated f=7.5cm, 1:4.5 focussing from 1m to infinity.

Shutter: Manually set between-the-lens type with speeds of 1/10 sec to 1/200 sec plus B, self timer, no flash synch.

Dates of Production: 1961.

Number Produced: ?

Serial Number Information: The camera serial number is located around the taking lens, on the shutter speed setting ring. The first two digits indicate the year of production.

Selling Price: ?

Features: A storage compartment with space for two filters is built into the left side of the body. It is covered by a swinging door.

Remarks: The thermoplastic bodied Changle is a faithful copy of the Russian Lubitel of the mid 1950s. It was made at the same time and in the same factory as the Hua Shan 35mm camera.

Hua Shan
(Hua Mountain)

Left: The Chinese Hua Shan and, right, the Russian Smena from which it was copied.

Factory: Xibei (Northwest) Optical Technical Factory.

Camera Type: Simple 35mm viewfinder camera.

Taking Lens: Coated three element, f=4cm, 1:4.5 front focussing, 1.3m to infinity.

Viewing Lens: Optical glass direct vision finder, showing field of view for 4cm lens.

Shutter: Manually set behind-the-lens leaf shutter with speeds of 1/10 sec to 1/200 sec, plus B, no self timer, no flash synch.

Dates of Production: 1960-61?

Number Produced: ?

Serial Number Information: The camera serial number is found around the lens. The first two digits indicate the year of manufacture.

Selling Price: 100 RMB yuan, with case.

Features: Accessory shoe and frame counter on the top plate.

Remarks: This thermoplastic 35mm camera is the same in every respect as the Yangtze River camera made earlier in Chongqing. It is a direct result of the co-operation between the Chinese and the Russians. This can be seen not only by the fact that both the Hua Shan and Yangtze River are identical to the Russian Smena camera, but also from the inverted 'U' on the lens, the cyrilic symbol denoting a coated lens.

Chang Jiang (Yangtze River)

The Chang Jiang, exactly the same as the Hua Shan which, in turn, is a copy of the Russian Smena camera.

Factory: Yangtze Government Electrical Factory, Chongqing, Sichuan.

Camera Type: Simple viewfinder camera.

Taking Lens: Coated three element, f=4cm, 1:4.5 front focussing, 1.3m to infinity.

Viewing Lens: Optical glass direct vision finder, showing field of view for 4cm lens.

Shutter: Manually set behind the lens leaf shutter with speeds of 1/10 sec to 1/200 sec, plus B, no self timer, no flash synch.

Dates of Production: 1958-60?

Number Produced: ?

Serial Number Information: The camera serial number is found around the lens. The first two digits may indicate the year of manufacture.

Selling Price: 100 RMB yuan?

Features: Accessory shoe on the top plate.

Remarks: This thermoplastic 35mm camera is the same in every respect as the Hua Shan made later in the Xibei Optical Technical Factory. It is the direct result of co-operation between the Chinese and the Russians. This can be seen not only by the fact that both the Hua Shan and Yangtze River are identical to the Russian Smena camera, but also from the inverted 'U' on the lens, the cyrilic symbol denoting a coated lens.

TH-2 Taihu
(Tai Lake)

Factory: Wuxi Camera Factory, Jiangsu Province, (though not marked on the camera).

Camera Type: Rangefinder with fixed lens.

Taking Lens: Coated f=50mm, 1:2.8 focussing 0.8m to infinity. Focussing scale in meters and feet.

Viewing Lens: Split-image rangefinder with field of view for 50mm lens.

Shutter: Between-the-lens type with speeds of 1 sec to 1/300 plus B, self timer, PC flash synch on body. Shutter cocking coupled to film advance.

Dates of Production: ?

Number Produced: ?

Serial Number Information: The serial number is located around the lens. The body does not have a number.

Selling Price: ?

Features: This mechanical 35mm camera offers an accessory shoe centered on the top plate, and a film reminder built into the lens housing, marked for ASA and DIN. A film plane

The Taihu, a 35mm rangefinder camera that was a screw-for-screw copy of the Seagull 205.

indicator is marked on the top plate. (The same as the Shanghai 205 and Seagull 205).

Remarks: The rear door for this camera is released by pulling on the film rewind knob, unlike the release button for the Shanghai 205, which is located on the bottom plate. The Taihu TH-2 is a good example of technology exchange between Chinese factories. This camera is screw for screw the twin of the Seagull 205.

Lao Dong
(Labour)

Front and back... the Lao Dong camera. Note the twin windows for 12 or 16 exposures.

Factory: Shanghai Guan Long Camera Material Store, Shanghai.

Camera Type: Simple 120 rollfilm viewfinder camera.

Taking Lens: Uncoated fixed focus from 1.6m to infinity.

Viewing Lens: Direct vision eye-level optical finder.

Shutter: Between-the-lens type with speeds of 1/25 sec and B, no self timer, no flash synch.

Dates of Production: 1958-60?

Number Produced: ?

Serial Number Information: No serial number appeared on this camera.

Selling Price: 39 RMB yuan.

Features: 12 exposures 6 x 6cm, or 16 exposures 6 x 4.5cm on 120 rollfilm.

Remarks: A copy of the Japanese Fujipet, the inexpensive Lao Dong camera was meant to fill in as an alternative to the more expensive and sophisticated TLRs and folding 120 cameras of the day. It had slight success in sales in the Shanghai area. Because of its cheap plastic and metal construction, few Lao Dong cameras exist today.

Unknown copy camera

Factory: ? (somewhere in China).

Camera Type: Special purpose copy camera, including copyboard base and built-in tungsten lighting.

Taking Lens: Coated f=30mm, 1:5.6, but only opening from f/8. 35mm screw thread mount. Focussing from about 0.75m down to about 0.33m, by use of numbers 1-4, corresponding to marked areas on the copy board.

Viewing Lens: No viewing system.

Shutter: Metal focal plane shutter with speeds of 1 sec to 1/20 sec plus B. No self timer, some were made with X flash synch, others had no synch. A cable release is needed to fire the shutter.

Dates of Production: ?

Number Produced: ?

Serial Number Information: The camera serial number is stamped on the interior of the body housing. It is not visible without disassembly of the camera. The same number is stamped into the combination carrying case/copy stand. No numbers higher than 111 have been seen. The lens has its own number around the lens bezel.

Selling Price: ?

Features: Built-in knife, removable long rollfilm holders, 18 x 24mm frame size,

Top, front and back... an unknown half-frame copy camera. Note the Chinese character for 'knife' on the top plate.

the earliest ones used knob advance, while later cameras had a trigger type advance.

Remarks: This 'noname' camera is the only known example of a half frame camera made in China. It was used to produce film strips for educational purposes. It was sold as part of a copy set, including its own light source for 110 or 220 volts.

Lanjiang (Blue Sword)

Factory: Tianjin Photographic Equipment Factory, Tianjin.

Camera Type: 360 degree panoramic camera.

Taking Lens: Coated f=240mm, 1:4.5, or f=360mm, 1:5.6, in screw mount flange in lens board.

Viewing Lens: Removable ground glass back.

Shutter: Slit type shutter, speeds are varied by rate at which the camera rotates, passing film by the opening in the opposite direction.

Dates of Production: 1970-85.

Number Produced: ?

Serial Number Information: No serial number information is available.

Selling Price: 6,000-8,000 RMB yuan, including carrying case, two lenses, nicad battery pack, and tripod.

Features: The rotation of the camera can be controlled to include 360 degrees. An electric motor drives the camera and film. A nicad battery pack is located under the camera, attached to the tripod, for use as a power source.

Remarks: ASA 100, 8-inch wide black and white film is still available, and comes bulk packed in cans containing 100m. The largest number of people sitting for a panoramic photo in Beijing was 700. The Chinese still have a fascination for panoramic group shots, though no panoramic scenes seem to be available. The Lanjiang is no longer made, and since it is still in daily use by studios, doesn't come on the market very often. Recent moves by foreign manufacturers to sell 120 rollfilm panoramic cameras have met with little success. The Chinese insist on the sharpness of the 8-inch wide black and white negative.

203mm Panoramic Camera

Factory: Shanghai Yong Feng Film Camera Factory Shanghai.

Camera Type: Folding panoramic camera, using 8-inch film, and electric drive.

Taking Lens: Coated f=240mm, 1:4.5, and f=360mm, 1:4.5 interchangeable lenses.

Viewing Lens: Ground glass focussing.

Shutter: Rotating slit type with speeds of 1/20 sec to 1/150 sec.

Dates of Production: 1987-present.

Number Produced: ?

Serial Number Information: No serial number information is available.

Selling Price: 10,000 RMB yuan with two lenses, carrying case, and tripod with power source and electric motor drive.

Features: Panoramic sweep variable up to 360 degrees. At 360 degrees the 240mm lens yields an 8 x 64 inch negative, while the 360mm lens gives an 8 x 98 inch film strip. Large cassettes are used for film loading, and allow changing film with greater ease than with Cirkut cameras.

Remarks: The Chinese are still enamoured by the large group shots familiar to us from the 1920s. This plastic bodied camera is meant to replace the No.8 Cirkut cameras with Turner-Reich triple convertible lenses, which are still in everyday use in larger Chinese cities. It is too early to tell if this camera will be a marketing success. It uses only black and white film, and since the Chinese public has recently fallen in love with colour, the chances seem slim.

YC-75X100*

The YC 75x100 instant picture camera. It took the form of a twin lens reflex with an electronically set shutter speed.

Factory: Shanghai Cine and Still Camera Research Institute Factory, Shanghai.

Camera Type: Instant picture twin lens reflex.

Taking Lens: Coated f=110mm, 1:8, stopping down to f/16.

Viewing Lens: Coated f=110mm, 1:8.

Shutter: Electrically controlled between-the-lens leaf type, imported from Japan, operating in the range of EV9 to EV15.

Dates of Production: 1980-82.

Number Produced: 200.

Serial Number Information: Body serial number is located inside the camera, stamped into the metal.

Selling Price: 4000 RMB yuan in 1980. In June of 1988 there were still ten unsold cameras at the factory, and they were available for 2500 RMB yuan.

Features: Reflex viewing on the 75mm x 100mm picture area. Shutter speed set electronically.

Remarks: This instant camera was a failure in several respects. It weighed more than ten pounds, and cost more than US$1,000. The instant film used provided no negative, and was of poor quality. It is said that film is still available.

***From the Chinese meaning 'at once', and the size of the delivered print.**

Greatwall DFA-CL

Factory: North China Optical Instrument Factory, Beijing.

Camera Type: 35mm Single lens reflex with built-in light meter.

Taking Lens: Coated f=58mm, 1:2.0 (Seagull DF design) in Nikon bayonette mount.

Viewing Lens: Reflex viewing with fixed ground glass focussing screen.

Shutter: Vertical metal focal plane type with speeds of 1 sec to 1/1000 sec, plus B. Self timer and M and X PC flash synch, plus hot shoe.

Dates of Production: 1975.

Number Produced: 4 (though parts for 10 were made).

Serial Number Information: The body number appears on the back of the top plate, and begins 26000X, the 26 being the number of years after liberation that the camera was produced. The lens carries it own number, also beginning 26000X, but not necessarily the same number as the camera.

Selling Price: About 670 RMB yuan was the planned selling price. The factory based this price on a comparison with the Seagull DF-1 of 1975 at 470 RMB yuan. Their feeling was that the addition of an internal light meter added 200 RMB yuan to the value of their camera.

The Greatwall DFA-CL, a copy of the Japanese Nikkormat FTN.

Features: Mirror lock-up, hotshoe, depth of field preview, available in black or chrome.

Remarks: Though made in Beijing, and carrying the Greatwall name, this camera has nothing to do with the Beijing Camera Factory. The North China Optical Instrument factory started in 1960 as a military factory making instruments for the Chinese army. 1975 was its first attempt at making a camera. After questioning the Chinese press about what they needed and wanted, the Nikkormat FTN was chosen to copy. The result was the DFA-CL. (CL standing for automatic light metering). Though the test was considered a success, the more than 1,000,000,000 RMB yuan needed to begin production was not available.

Tian Chi
(Heavenly Pond)

Factory: Chang Chun Optical Research Institute, Jilin Province.

Camera Type: 35mm single lens reflex.

Taking Lens: Coated, 56mm, f=1:1.9, focussing from 6m to infinity.

Viewing Lens: Fixed pentaprism, ground glass with central split-image rangefinder.

Shutter: Cloth focal plane type with speeds of 1 sec to 1/1000 sec plus B, self timer and flash synch.

Dates of Production: 1959 only.

Number Produced: 10.

Serial Number Information: Body serial numbers begin with 50XXXXX, while lens serial numbers begin 30XXXXX.

Selling Price: Never sold on the market.

Features: The first Chinese camera with automatic aperture, stopping down at the moment of exposure. A breech type mount was used, similar to that on Canon SLR cameras.

Remarks: Produced in honour of the tenth anniversary of the founding of the People's Republic of China, the Tian Chi

The Tian Chi SLR, a close copy of the Contax S from East Germany.

is another example of technology in China failing. A copy of the Contax S, from East Germany, the ten cameras which were made all stayed in the Institute where they were made. Eight of the original number have been broken, and discarded, the eighth one falling victim to a detachment of Red Guards during the Cultural Revolution. Two cameras remain, one currently at the Institute, and another in the hands of a Chinese student studying in the United States. I was offered this student's camera for 500$US, when I took the photographs of it used in this book. The student never phoned me back to arrange the sale.

Hong Qi (Red Flag)

Factory: Gansu Optical Research Institute Factory, Gansu Province.

Camera Type: Mechanical 16mm silent cine camera.

Taking Lens: 16mm f=1:1.9, 25mm f=1:1.5, and 50mm f=1:1.6, all coated, and mounted on camera in a rotating turret.

Viewing Lens: Through-the-lens viewing, using a beam splitter in front of the shutter. Dioptre adjustment on the eyepiece.

Shutter: Metal rotary type with adjustments for 12, 16, 24, and 36 frames/second. One full winding of the spring motor works allows about 40 seconds of continuous filming at 16 frames/second.

Dates of Production: 1980?

Number Produced: ?

Serial Number Information: The camera serial number is located inside the loading door with the first two digits being the year of production. Each lens also has a serial number located on the lens bezel, the first two digits also indicate year of production.

Selling Price: ?

Features: Interchangeable lenses, shutter release lock. Frames/second cannot be changed without removing a

The Red Flag 16mm movie camera, originally inspired by the Bolex.

clear plastic screw cover over the adjustment dial. The characters used on the camera are of the same handwriting as those used on the Red Flag 20 camera from Shanghai. The style is that of Chairman Mao.

Remarks: While no figures can be given for the amount of Red Flag cine cameras made, the total must certainly be fewer than 500. This camera is well built, and comes with a hard leather system case. It is said that the Red Flag is a copy of a Russian copy of a Bolex camera, but this has not been confirmed.

Hong Mei HM-1 (Red Plum Blossom)

Factory: Changzhou Camera Factory, Changzhou.

Camera Type: Folding 120 viewfinder camera, with scale focussing.

Taking Lens: Coated 5cm, 1:4.5, three elements in three groups, with scale focussing from 1.5m to infinity.

Shutter: Manually set between-the-lens type. 1/10 sec to 1/200 sec plus B, self timer and PC synch.

Dates of Production: ?

Number Produced: ?

Serial Number Information: The camera serial number appears inside the body, stamped in ink on a piece of paper, glued to the back door.

Selling Price: 65 RMB yuan, with case, recently discounted to 45 RMB yuan.

The Hong Mei HM-1, a folding rollfilm camera that remained popular for many years, although now out of production.

Features: Shutter release coupled to body. Hinged masks built into the body for 6 x 6 or 6 x 4.5 on 120 rollfilm. Ruby window frame counting, marked for 12 and 16 frames. No double exposure prevention. Accessory shoe on top plate.

Remarks: This folding 120 camera was very popular a few years ago. It filled the market left vacant when the Shanghai 202 ceased production. Though now out of production, it still can be found new on many smaller camera store shelves.

Hong Mei-3
(Red Plum Blossom)

Factory: Changzhou Camera Factory.

Camera Type: 120 folding rollfilm camera.

Taking Lens: Coated three elements in three groups Cooke type lens. f/3.5, 75mm, focussing from 1.2m to infinity. Lenses were made under sub-contract at the Beijing Camera Factory.

Viewing Lens: Combined rangefinder/ viewfinder window, no frame lines for 6 x 4.5cm field of view.

Shutter: Manually set between-the-lens type with speeds of 1 sec to 1/300 sec, plus B, post type flash synch, self timer.

Dates of Production: 1984?

Number produced: Less than 1,000

Serial Number Information: This camera has no serial number, either on the lens, or on the camera body, though numbers written in pencil were used to identify parts made for particular cameras.

Selling Price: Sold in test market in the Shanghai area for 65 RMB yuan.

Features: Accessory shoe on the top plate, hinged flaps used to create 16, 6 x 4.5cm, or 12, 6 x 6cm exposures on

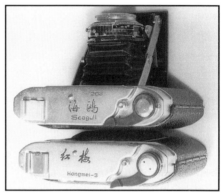

The second version of the Seagull 203, compared to the Hong Mei-3

120 rollfilm, by use of two red windows. Provision for coupled rangefinder.

Remarks: Produced in quantities for the test market only, the Hong Mei-3 camera was designed to compete with the Seagull 203, at a time when the latter was being phased out of production by the Shanghai Camera Factory. The prototype pictured does not contain either a rangefinder, or the necessary rangefinder-to-lens connections, though attachment holes are drilled and tapped. Unlike the Seagull 203, which it otherwise copies very closely, the Hong Mei-3 has no film advance indicator. This hand-made camera came at the wrong time. The advent of imported minilabs killed the call for 120 rollfilm cameras.

Hongmei 5

The Hongmei 5 twin lens reflex, made mostly from polystyrene plastic.

Factory: Changzhou Camera Factory, Changzhou.

Camera Type: Twin Lens Reflex.

Taking Lens: Coated f=75mm, 1:4.5, focussing from 1.2m to infinity.

Viewing Lens: Unmarked.

Shutter: Manually set between-the-lens type with speeds of 1/10 sec to 1/200 sec plus B, self timer, PC type flash synch.

Dates of Production: ?

Number Produced: ?

Serial Number Information: The serial number is located inside the back door, printed on a piece of paper glued inside.

Selling Price: 85 RMB yuan, with case.

Features: Fresnel focussing screen with central ground spot. Focussing by means of a lever under the taking lens. 12 exposures 6 x 6cm, or 16 exposures 6 x 4.5cm on 120 rollfilm.

Remarks: The lightweight Hongmei 5 is made mostly of polystyrene plastic. Only the lens and shutter assembly and some small sheetmetal parts and screws are metal. Though the viewing lens is not marked, it appears to be of 1: 3.5 size. The taking lens and shutter are the same as used on the Hongmei 1 folding camera.

Zhe Jiang 201 (Pearl River-201)

Camera Factory: Sichuan Province.

Camera Type: 35mm SLR.

Taking Lens: Coated f=50mm 1:2.0 focussing from 0.45m to infinity.

Viewing Lens: Removable pentaprism ground glass with central microprism and split image rangefinder.

Shutter: Mechanical horizontal cloth focal plane shutter with speeds of 1 sec to 1/1000 sec. X flash synch at 1/45 sec self timer.

Dates of Production: 1979 - present?

Number Produced: Tens of thousands.

Serial Number Information: The body number appears on the top plate, under the film rewind. A second number giving the year of manufacture is visible on the body casting when the pentaprism is removed. The lens has its own number around the lens bezel.

Selling Price: 690 RMB yuan.

Features: Mirror lock-up. Removable pentaprism, removable accessory shoe, which attaches to the rewind knob, black professional finish.

The Zhe Jiang 201... the most expensive of the mechanical Chinese-produced 35mm single lens reflexes.

Remarks: The Pearl River 35mm camera uses the Minolta MD lens mounting system featured on the Seagull DF-1. Though the most expensive of the mechanical Chinese-produced 35mm SLRs, this camera is very popular, and is often seen swinging from the necks of Chinese touring the Great Wall.

Photoing On Car

The Photoing On Car. It has been seen in the West and was thought to have been made in the 1950s.

Factory: Somewhere in China.

Camera Type: Plastic, with built in flash.

Taking Lens: Uncoated opaque type.

Viewing Lens: Maybe.

Shutter: Yes.

Dates of Production: 1980s or earlier.

Number produced: Lots.

Serial Number Information: No serial number is to be seen on this camera, though the car itself might be affixed with a number plate.

Selling Price: 21.30 RMB yuan, with cardboard box, two D batteries required, not included.

Features: Red convertible included in price of camera.

Remarks: The Photoing On Car camera has been seen in the West, and had thought to have been made in the 1950s. Recently it was found on a store shelf in Beijing. Approximately 40% of the Photoing On Car cameras on the store shelf were non-functional. Possibly autofocus, this camera is very economical to operate, as it needs no film.

Index